Wild About the Okavango

ALL-IN-ONE GUIDE TO
COMMON ANIMALS & PLANTS
OF THE OKAVANGO DELTA,
CHOBE NATIONAL PARK AND CAPRIVI STRIP

Duncan Butchart

SOUTHERN
BOOK PUBLISHERS

*D*edicated to the memory of Rick Lomba,
whose passion for the Okavango Delta
continues to inspire many who strive for the
conservation of this unique wilderness.

Acknowledgements

Many friends and colleagues have assisted me in the compilation of this book and their
support is greatly appreciated. Valuable comments on the introductory sections were
provided by Fred Ellery and Ann Cameron. Individual sections were read by specialists
in their fields: John and Sandie Burrows, and Fred and Karen Ellery (plants), Vincent
Carruthers (frogs), Dr Paul Skelton (fishes) and Buster Culverwell (reptiles); any errors
are, however, of my own making. The names of the photographers who supplied material
additional to my own are listed alongside their respective pictures. I am particularly
grateful to Colin Bell, Lex Hes, Vincent Carruthers, Paul Skelton, Peter Lawson, and
Chris and Tilde Stuart for their generous provision of photographs, and to James
Marshall for the loan of photographic equipment. Brendan Ryan and John Carlyon kindly
permitted the use of photographs at a reduced rate. Ian Adam led a Mondeor High School
expedition to the Okavango Delta in 1976 – a trip which sparked off my interest in the
region. Subsequent explorations have been greatly enhanced by the friendship and
knowledge of Colin Bell, Buster Culverwell, Dave Lincoln, Keith Stannard, Dave
Hamman, Ed White and Louise England, James Marshall, Mark Tennant, Marie
Holstenson and Grant Burton. Observations by Cecil and Shelagh Peterson were of value
in finalising the list of featured birds. I am grateful to Southern Book Publishers for their
belief in the 'Wild About' series, and in particular to Louise Grantham for her enthusiasm
and Mike Thayer for his assistance. Finally, I thank my wife Tracey for helping in
numerous ways, and for her love, support and encouragement.

ISBN: 1 86812 594 7

First edition, first impression 1995

Published by
Southern Book Publishers (Pty) Ltd
PO Box 3103, Halfway House 1685, South Africa

Design and typesetting by Groundhog Graphics, Nelspruit
Reproduction by Hirt & Carter, Cape Town
Printed and bound by National Book Printers, Drukkery Street, Goodwood, Western Cape.

Contents

INTRODUCTION   2
HOW TO USE THIS GUIDE   4
GEOLOGY AND TOPOGRAPHY   5
MAP OF REGION   6
CLIMATE   9
IDENTIFYING AND WATCHING WILDLIFE   10
HABITAT DESCRIPTIONS   11
    Open Water   12
    Permanent Swamp   13
    Floodplain Grasslands   14
    Islands   15
    Riverine Forest   16
    Savanna and Scrub   17
    Woodland   18
    Rocky Outcrops   19
SPECIES DESCRIPTIONS
    Mammals   20
    Birds   34
    Reptiles   84
    Frogs   91
    Freshwater Fishes   95
    Invertebrates   100
    Trees and Woody Shrubs   106
    Soft-stemmed Shrubs and Herbs   118
    Grasses and Sedges   121
REFERENCES AND FURTHER READING   122
DESTINATIONS AND USEFUL ADDRESSES   123
GLOSSARY OF SCIENTIFIC TERMS   123
INDEX OF FEATURED SPECIES   124

INTRODUCTION

Unlike most rivers, the Okavango – which has its source in the highlands of central Angola – never reaches the sea. Instead it spills out onto the sands of the Kalahari Basin to create an oasis in the desert. The mosaic of channels, islands, lagoons and forests that have resulted support a wealth of wildlife including large carnivores, great herds of elephant and spectacular birds.

This book is intended to fill a perceived niche for a simple, compact guide to the more common birds, mammals, fishes, plants and other forms of wildlife found in the region, and also to emphasise the interrelatedness of these life forms. It does not attempt to be comprehensive as there already exist a number of publications which focus in detail on individual groups of southern African animals and plants. For similar reasons this is not a 'where to go' book, although a map of the area showing places of interest, is included.

For reasons of ecological similarity, the area covered by this guide extends beyond the Okavango Delta to incorporate the Kwando-Linyanti-Chobe wetlands to the north, the Chobe National Park to the east, and the Tsodilo Hills and surrounding broad-leaved woodlands in the west. Many larger mammals – in particular African Elephant and Burchell's Zebra – move on a seasonal basis across this vast region of approximately 120 000 km². Although abutting the area in the south, Nxai Pan and the Makgadikgadi Pans are not included as the flora and fauna here are markedly different, being typical of the arid Kalahari.

Major conservation areas are the Moremi Game Reserve and Chobe National Park in Botswana, and Mudumo, Mamile and Mahango national parks in Namibia. All of these reserves may be visited with four-wheel drive vehicles or, in the case of the first three, as a guest at a private camp. Extensive Wildlife Management Areas (WMAs) – where the utilisation of wildlife, including trophy hunting, is the primary form of land use – exist alongside Moremi and Chobe in Botswana.

The Okavango region is populated by an ethnically diverse people, including original Khoisan-speaking inhabitants – the Basarwa – who are now in the minority. Bantu tribes include the Batawana, Hambukushu, Herero and Bayei, most of whom speak Setswana. A small number of people of European ancestry, many of whom are citizens of Botswana, have also chosen to settle in the beautiful surroundings. In East Caprivi, Khoisan-speaking Barekwena are numbered among the diverse population dominated by Bantu-speaking peoples, many being related to the Lozi of Zambia. Recent estimates put the combined population of the Okavango-Chobe-East Caprivi region at about 150 000, with the majority centered in towns such as Maun, Kasane and Katima Mulilo. In the reality of the modern world these people are as much a part of the environment as the wildlife, the future of which lies in their hands. Conservation in Africa will only succeed if local communities are themselves involved in the management of wildlife resources and derive tangible benefits from tourism. In this regard it should be noted that the Moremi Wildlife Reserve was the first of its kind to be established by non-colonial administrators in Africa – the Batawana tribe set aside the land in 1962.

No book on the Okavango Delta – not even a field guide such as this – can rightfully ignore the threats which this unique wilderness faces. Although visitors will be enthralled by the apparently unspoiled nature of the landscapes, they should also be aware that a number of subtle and pervasive factors threaten the delicate ecological balance which has evolved over the millennia. Much has been said about the negative effects – actual and likely – of water extraction, insecticide spraying in tsetse fly control, abuse of hunting licenses, cordon fences aimed at separating cattle from wildlife, invasion of alien plants and the encroachment onto floodplains by growing herds of cattle. Whatever point of view one may take on these and other relevant issues, it must be accepted that the Botswana Government is in an unenviable situation, in that the Delta – its greatest long-term asset – is also the only sizeable source of water in an arid country hungry for development.

I first visited the Okavango Delta in September 1976 on a school expedition. It took four days to negotiate the rugged road through the Kalahari, north of South Africa – in vehicles ill-suited for the trip – before our group reached the frontier town of Maun. Parched, dust-covered and filled with anticipation, we drank and splashed in the crystal clear waters of the Delta much as thirsty antelope do after trekking for miles. Like many before and since, I became captivated by this magnificent wilderness, and have returned whenever possible. It is my hope that this book will provide added awareness of the great wealth which Botswana holds in her hands.

HOW TO USE THIS GUIDE

The animals and plants

Most of the animals which you are likely to see in the region are included, with an emphasis on mammals, birds and fishes – the groups of greatest interest to most visitors. Species are arranged in such a way that those with similar characteristics are together, even though this sequence may differ from standard reference works. In addition to the species featured, mention is made of less common similar species (ss) with which they might be confused. Due to limitations of space, invertebrates are not treated in any detail, but it is hoped that the information provided will create some awareness of this fascinating, and often hard to ignore, group of animals. Of the plants, only the larger trees are treated in any detail, although many of the important aquatic plants are also covered. Alien (non-indigenous) species are few, but those which do occur are marked with an asterisk (*).

The names of species follow those of the most recent authoritative publications, but in line with ornithological publications – and in order to standardise terminology in this guide – hyphens have been eliminated from all double-barrelled common names. The scientific names of trees and other plants are used ahead of common names, as the latter often differ from region to region, and frequently relate species to families to which they do not belong. The name of the family to which each featured plant belongs is included for this reason. The Tswana names of plants are provided where possible. Scientific terms have been kept to a minimum but could not be avoided altogether; an abbreviated glossary of these terms is provided on p. 123.

At the beginning of each section introductory notes provide general hints on identification, and the recognised reference books are listed. In addition to this, a list of books for further reading is provided on p. 122.

The habitats

Eight distinctive habitats, from permanent swamp to dry woodland, are identified and their characteristics described. Recognition of the habitat that you are in is an important aspect of identification as many species are specific to certain vegetation or soil types. Coded symbols link each species with the habitats in which it is most likely to be encountered.

The illustrations

The photographs have been chosen to best demonstrate key identification features. Where male and female of one species differ, the sex not illustrated is described in the text. In most cases, plants have been photographed in close-up, to best illustrate leaves, flowers or fruit. Some difficult-to-photograph species are illustrated with colour paintings.

GEOLOGY AND TOPOGRAPHY

The lie-of-the-land, or general topography, is a direct result of the geological history of an area as well as processes such as erosion and deposition. These processes are often difficult to grasp by the non-specialist, however, and few people show much interest in the soil under their feet or the landforms around them. This is unfortunate, as these features reveal the processes responsible for landscape formation.

Two things are obvious when considering the geology and topography of the Okavango Delta region. Firstly, the area is so flat that termite mounds are the highest landforms (actually the land slopes gradually – 1 m every 4 km – to the south-east), and secondly, there are very few rocks, or even stones, to be seen (but see p. 19). The entire area lies within the Kalahari Basin – a great depression filled with wind-blown sands extending from the north-eastern corner of South Africa to just south of the equator in Zaire. The rocks underlying this sand are of sedimentary or volcanic origin.

Although the surface geology is simple, the rocks below the sands are seismically active and the area is prone to earthquakes. The last major quake was in 1952 and measured 6.7 on the Richter Scale.

Formation of the Okavango Delta

In years gone by the Okavango River was thought to have reached the sea, but various authors differ on how, and even into which ocean, it flowed. Some believe that it joined the Limpopo River, while others speculate that it met the Orange River. Wherever it flowed in the past, the situation changed when tectonic movement gave rise to a series of parallel faults (see map on pp. 6 and 7) which caused a segment of the Earth's crust to collapse. Trapped within the confines of these so-called graben faults – considered to be a south-eastern extension of Africa's Great Rift Valley – the course of the Okavango was interrupted, leading to the formation of an inland delta or, to be geographically correct, an alluvial fan.

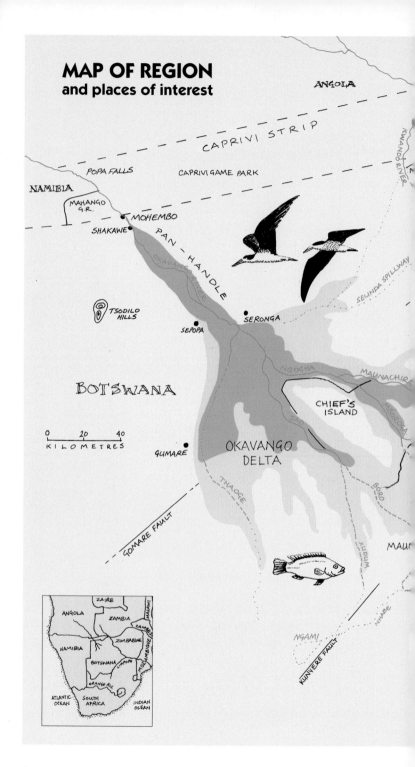

MAP OF REGION
and places of interest

ANGOLA

CAPRIVI STRIP

CAPRIVI GAME PARK

POPA FALLS

KWANDO RIVER

NAMIBIA

MAHANGO G.R.

MOHEMBO

SHAKAWE

PAN - HANDLE

OKAVANGO RIVER

SELINDA SPILLWAY

TSODILO HILLS

SERONGA

SEPOPA

BOTSWANA

NQOGHA

MAUNACHIRA

CHIEF'S ISLAND

NQOGHA

0   20   40
K I L O M E T R E S

GUMARE

ZAO

OKAVANGO DELTA

BORO

THAOGE

GOMARE FAULT

MAUI

WHDHA

ZAIRE

ANGOLA   ZAMBIA   MALAWI

NAMIBIA   ZAMBEZI   ZIMBABWE   MOZAMBIQUE

BOTSWANA   LIMPOPO

ATLANTIC OCEAN   ORANGE RIV.

SOUTH AFRICA   INDIAN OCEAN

NGAMI

NHABE

KUNYERE FAULT

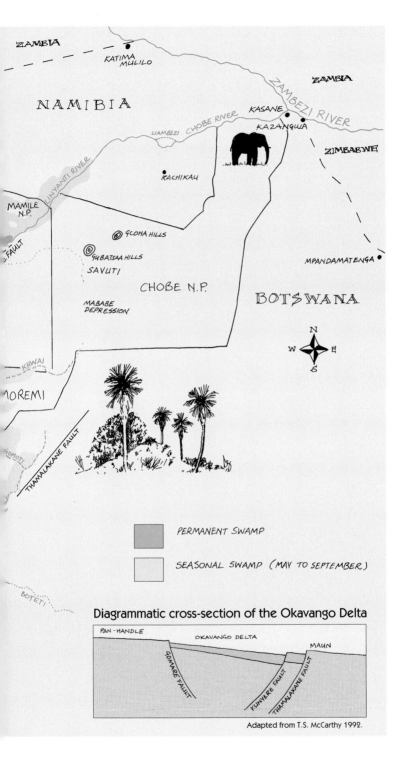

ZAMBIA

KATIMA
MULILO

ZAMBIA

NAMIBIA

ZAMBEZI RIVER

KASANE

LIAMBEZI CHOBE RIVER

KAZANGULA

ZIMBABWE

LINYANTI RIVER

KACHIKAU

MAMILE
N.P.

FAULT

GCOHA HILLS

GUBATSAA HILLS

SAVUTI

MPANDAMATENGA

CHOBE N.P.

BOTSWANA

MABABE
DEPRESSION

N

W   E

S

KHWAI

MOREMI

THAMALAKANE FAULT

GOMOTI

PERMANENT SWAMP

SEASONAL SWAMP (MAY TO SEPTEMBER)

BOTETI

Diagrammatic cross-section of the Okavango Delta

PAN-HANDLE

OKAVANGO DELTA

MAUN

GOMARE FAULT

KUNYERE FAULT

THAMALAKANE FAULT

Adapted from T.S. McCarthy 1992.

7

Components and dynamics of the Okavango Delta

The Okavango Delta consists of three major components, and one way of picturing this is to look at your outstretched hand. The wrist is the **'pan-handle'**, the palm the **permanent swamp**, and the fingers the channels – arteries which feed the **seasonal swamp**. This environment fluctuates between wet and dry seasons with the summer rains of the catchment reaching the base of the Delta in the rain-free winter months.

The Okavango River enters Botswana at Mohembo, having travelled some 1 000 km from its source, and is channelled through a 15 km-wide 'corridor' between two secondary faults. This is the so-called **'pan-handle'** and the river meanders through a papyrus-filled swamp, between banks of compacted sand and peat. The floodwater peak at Mohembo is in March or April, and the river depth fluctuates by up to two metres.

Just past the village of Seronga, the river crosses the Gomare Fault. No sand banks contain the flow here, and the water flows into three main channels. The Nqogha-Maunachira-Mboroga-Santantadibe System drains to the east, the Jao-Boro System down the centre and the Thaoge to the south along the western side of the Delta. The upper reaches of these channel systems are permanently flooded, as is the land immediately adjacent to the first two systems for much of their length. The Thaoge began choking up with vegetation at the turn of the century, and now has a severely limited flow. This area of some 6 000 km² is known as the **permanent swamp**, and is typified by groves of Wild Date Palm *Phoenix reclinata*, beds of papyrus, islands rimmed with forest, and lagoons sprinkled with waterlilies.

Beyond the permanent swamp is an extensive area seasonally flooded between May and September. This region is fed with water by innumerable small channels, as well as by flow across and through reed beds. This **seasonal swamp** covers an area of up to 12 000 km², and is typified by open grasslands when the floodwaters recede, and shallow wetlands during the flood. Islands of all shapes and sizes are numerous. As floodwaters recede, islands become linked by land and depressions hold pans of water. The floodwaters flow only as far as the Kunyere and Thamalakane faults where they may back to a depth of two metres against the fault scarps. In years of exceptional floods, water may 'escape' via the Boteti River to evaporate in the desert, or flow towards the Mababe Depression or Lake Ngami (now an ephemeral pan).

The floodwaters move slowly through the network of channels and down the gentle gradient, taking about four months to travel the 250 km from Mohembo (at 1 000 m above sea level) to Maun (at 935 m). The average annual inflow of water into the Delta has been estimated at some 11 000 million m³, and this is augmented by some 5 000 million m³ of local rainfall. Over 90% of this water evaporates, but not before it has brought life and sustenance to the wildlife and people of the region.

The Kwando-Linyanti-Chobe System

The Kwando River begins its life as the Cuando in Angola, rising some 100 km east of the Cuito and Cubango (which together form the Okavango). As it turns eastwards, at the lowest point of Namibia's Caprivi Strip, it becomes the Linyanti and here forms a wetland similar to, but much smaller than, the Okavango Delta (the Gomare Fault is responsible for the back-up). Upon heading east again, the river is known as the Chobe, and forms the northern border of the Chobe National Park. Here the broad floodplain attracts great numbers of large mammals (in particular herds of African Elephant and Buffalo) as well as congregations of waterfowl. At Kazangula, the Chobe meets the Zambezi, some 60 km before the Victoria Falls in Zimbabwe.

Dryland environments

Not all of the area encompassed by this book is subject to permanent or seasonal flooding. To the west of the Okavango Delta, and beyond the Kwando River in Caprivi, deep Kalahari sands support vast tracts of tall Zambezi Teak *Baikiaea plurijuga* woodland. East of the Delta, and again along the fringes of the Kwando-Linyanti-Chobe River, compacted clay soils (alluvial deposits from a wetter era) are dominated by Mopane *Colophospermum mopane* woodland. The large Chief's Island, which lies in the centre of the Delta, is comprised mostly of clay and Mopane, although sandy soils with different vegetation occur along its perimeter. The old 'marsh' of Savuti – once an overflow from the Linyanti – now supports highly nutritious grasses, attractive to grazing herbivores.

Three agents play a vital role in the shaping of dryland environments: **fire** – a frequent occurrence in the dry winter months – keeps areas open by removing tree and shrub saplings; **elephants** modify woodlands, turning them into open areas by felling large trees; and **termites** create raised ground through their mound-building activities, providing sites for tree and shrub colonisation out of reach of fire and flood.

CLIMATE

Northern Botswana and the adjacent Caprivi are in the sub-tropics, with temperatures and rainfall fluctuating markedly between the seasons. The average daytime temperature in midsummer (December-January) is about 32 °C (max. 42 °C), dropping to about 18 °C at night. In midwinter (June-July) the daily average is 25 °C, dropping to 5 or 6 °C at night. Only occasionally do temperatures drop below freezing, and frost is rare.

Rainfall at Maun, at the base of the Okavango Delta, averages 500 mm per year, but this figure increases progressively to the north. Almost all rain falls between November and April, usually in thundershowers. Humidity may be high in summer, but is extremely low in winter. Drought appears to be a cyclical phenomenon.

IDENTIFYING AND WATCHING WILDLIFE

Due to the occurrence of potentially dangerous large mammals, exploration of the wildlife reserves of the Okavango region can only be done by vehicle, or in some instances, on supervised walking trails from private camps. Although being in a vehicle has its limitations, there are also advantages as most animals, including birds, are less concerned about vehicles than they are about people, and often allow a closer approach. This is especially true of the well-used tourist routes. Photography is also far easier from a vehicle which acts as a hide and provides a higher vantage point. Travelling by vehicle is best in the early mornings and late afternoons, when animals are more active. In the dry winter months, parking at a pan or waterhole and simply waiting is one of the most rewarding ways of seeing wildlife.

By far the best – and often the only – way of getting about in the Delta itself is by dug-out canoe (*mokoro*). These craft, piloted by experienced polers, slip silently through waterways, enabling you to see aquatic flora and fauna at duck level. Powerboats are noisy and disruptive to certain forms of wildlife, but this method of transport is necessary in some cases (to reach particular camps, for instance) and an experienced pilot can ensure that the environment is not harmed.

Birds, and smaller creatures such as bats, reptiles, frogs and insects, are often common around lodges and camp sites, and it is wise to spend time exploring these surroundings on foot, although one should be careful not to venture out of sight of staff or companions. Trees and other plants are best studied in such places where leaves, bark and flowers can be examined.

At certain public campsites, arch-opportunists in the form of Chacma Baboon, Vervet Monkey and Spotted Hyena have become a nuisance as thoughtless people leave food unattended, or directly feed the animals. Once these animals are accustomed to being fed, they may become aggressive and dangerous, and will ultimately have to be destroyed by park authorities.

Before setting out, make yourself familiar with the species which you are likely to see by studying this book and others. The habitat symbols alongside the species accounts in this book will guide you to the places where you are most likely to find certain animals and plants. Keeping a diary or notebook is invaluable, but don't be shy to make written notes in your field guides – including this one – as these will be of use later for the rapid identification of the same or similar species.

Consideration for wildlife should always take priority. Drive or walk slowly so as not to disturb the animals you hope to see. If you are in an open vehicle avoid sudden movements and speak softly at all times. Getting close to a wild animal is a hollow achievement if you disrupt its life in the process.

HABITAT DESCRIPTIONS

Planet Earth can be divided into several broad categories of land type. Geographers refer to these as **vegetation zones**, and they include such well-known types as forest, grassland and desert. Recognising the interrelatedness of all life forms, ecologists now prefer to use the word **biome** for these broad definitions so as to embrace all the components. Generally speaking, particular plants and animals are characteristic of, and confined to, a particular biome, but there are notable exceptions, particularly among birds and larger mammals.

A biome is determined by **geology** and **climate** and although mankind may modify or even destroy the landscape, its classification does not change. Within each biome, various factors – such as local rainfall, soil type and aspect – give rise to distinct **habitats**.

The area covered by this book falls within the **savanna-woodland biome** but, as already mentioned, much of the landscape has been transformed by the Okavango Delta and its floodwaters. On the pages that follow, eight distinct habitats – from the permanent waters of rivers, channels and lagoons to the dry woodlands dominated by mopane or teak – are recognised. The characteristics of each are briefly described and some typical plants and animals mentioned. With a few exceptions, habitats rarely divide into neat blocks and a great deal of merging and overlap occurs. In such areas – known as **ecotones** – species diversity is often at its greatest.

The colour-coded symbols at the top of each habitat page are used throughout the species accounts as a means of linking the various animals and plants to their preferred habitat.

Key to habitat symbols

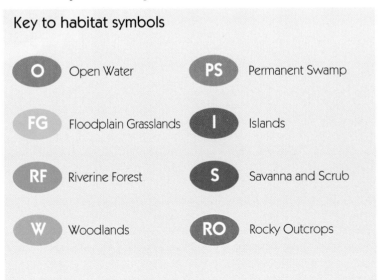

O — Open Water

PS — Permanent Swamp

FG — Floodplain Grasslands

I — Islands

RF — Riverine Forest

S — Savanna and Scrub

W — Woodlands

RO — Rocky Outcrops

Open Water

Two perennial rivers – the Okavango and the Kwando (later known as the Linyanti and Chobe) – drain from the north-west into the area. A third, the Zambezi (fourth largest on the continent), runs along the northern border of the Caprivi and is joined by the Chobe. These rivers are typically deep, slow-flowing and contained within solid banks.

Channels differ from rivers in that they are smaller and their flow is largely directed by vegetation such as papyrus. The major channel systems of the Okavango Delta have been discussed earlier, but numerous smaller channels radiate out across the Delta. All flow deepest and strongest in their upper reaches, petering out as they head south or east.

Lagoons (*madiba*) are small permanent lakes within the Delta, often where previous river systems meandered or formed ox-bows. Several channels may converge or disperse from lagoons. Lake Ngami and Lake Liambezi are now merely ephemeral pans destined to end up like the dry Mababe Depression (once a lake fed by the Savuti Channel).

Pans are seasonal, temporary bodies of water left behind in depressions on floodplains as floodwaters recede, or rain-filled pools in poorly drained clay soils associated with mopane woodland.

Among mammals, Hippo and Cape Clawless Otter spend most of their time in open water. Typical aquatic birds include Darter, Reed Cormorant, Pygmy Goose and African Fish Eagle. Bee-eaters, swifts, swallows and bats regularly forage for insects above water. The Nile Crocodile, Okavango Hinged Terrapin, various snakes, frogs and, of course, freshwater fishes are all aquatic. Typical plants include floating waterlilies.

Permanent Swamp

LEX HES

Areas permanently inundated with water are characteristic of the upper reaches of the Okavango Delta and the Linyanti Wetland. Overspill from the Okavango River in the so-called 'pan-handle', and also from the major channels, has created a swamp dominated by floating-leaved, submerged and emergent plant communities. Beneath this is a substrate varying from fine silt and sand to peat beds.

Of the **floating-leaved plants**, the Day Waterlily *Nymphaea nouchali* and Water Chestnut *Trapa natans* are most abundant. Communities of these plants are most common in deeper water along channel and lagoon fringes. African and Lesser Jacana, Painted Reed Frog and aquatic insects are typical.

Most distinctive of the **submerged plants** is the Water Lettuce *Ottelia ulvifolia* which has long, broad trailing leaves. Many fish, frogs and aquatic insects deposit their eggs on such plants.

Rooted emergent plants dominate the permanent swamp. Papyrus *Cyperus papyrus* – growing up to 5 m tall – is the most successful, and forms extensive, dense stands. Common Reed *Phragmites australis* and Bulrush *Typha capensis* also form dense stands, as does the tall grass *Miscanthus junceus* which grows in peat in the middle reaches of the Delta. These plants spread by means of rhizomes but are restrained by rapid water flow, fire and the movements of Hippo. Sitatunga, Greater Cane Rat, warblers, cisticolas and weavers are characteristic.

Colonies of tangled Swamp Fig *Ficus verruculosa* provide a suitable structure for the nests of herons, egrets, storks and cormorants. Often growing among these small fig trees are Waterberry *Syzygium cordatum* and colonies of the Swamp Fern *Thelypteris interrupta*.

Floodplain Grasslands

Much of the southern parts of the Okavango Delta and areas adjacent to the permanent swamps are seasonally inundated in midwinter when the extent of flooding is greatest. Unlike the permanent swamps, where water levels remain relatively constant, the appearance of the floodplain changes throughout the year, and from year to year depending upon rainfall in the catchment area. Tufted grass species such as *Panicum* and *Cymbopogon* dominate, with Couch Grass *Cynodon dactylon* on raised ground. Termite mounds and islands dot the floodplains. The grassy Mababe Depression, once a lake, is no longer flooded.

During winter, the floodplain is typically covered in shallow water with the grass cover being swept over and submerged. Waterlilies and other plants of the permanent swamps may invade the area, and provide additional cover for spawning fish. Red Lechwe, Wattled Crane, Slaty Egret, Longtoed Plover, and Mascarene Grass Frog are characteristic.

In spring and early summer, the floodwaters evaporate and slowly recede, and the exposed grass grows exuberantly. Herds of Buffalo, Tsessebe, Blue Wildebeest and Burchell's Zebra move in to feed. Cheetah are among the large carnivores which capitalise on this influx. Shoals of fish, including large numbers of Sharptooth Catfish (Barbel), often become stranded in shrinking pools where they attract gatherings of birds such as Marabou Stork, Yellowbilled Stork, African Spoonbill and various species of heron and egret.

As the grassland dries out, fierce fires often sweep the area, removing tree and shrub saplings in the process. Young woody plants cannot tolerate fire or waterlogging, which is why there is such a marked junction between floodplain grassland and other habitats.

Islands

Islands of various shapes and sizes are distributed throughout the Okavango Delta – in both the permanent and seasonal swamps – and contribute to the wondrous appearance of the landscape. By providing a constantly dry environment, these islands add to the diversity of life. In the flatness of the Okavango, any patch of raised ground may be considered an 'island' and they range in size from the large landmass of Chief's Island to a single termite mound.

Well-defined bands of vegetation are evident on most islands. Wild Date Palm *Phoenix reclinata* dominates the outer fringes while Sycamore Fig *Ficus sycomorus*, Jackalberry *Diospyros mespiliformis* and Knobthorn *Acacia nigrescens* are among the trees which form a forest behind. Ivory Palm *Hyphaene petersiana* grows as thickets or elegant giants in the island interior, much of which may be covered in Couch Grass *Cynodon dactylon* or Spike Grass *Sporobolus spicatus*. Water Mongoose, Pel's Fishing Owl, Heuglin's Robin and Water Monitor are typical of smaller islands, while larger landmasses may be home to all manner of wildlife including African Elephant and Lion.

Islands are formed in a variety of ways. Smaller, circular islands originate from termite mounds, while sinuous islands are the result of raised channel beds caused by channel abandonment through blockage. Islands expand by a process of chemical precipitation which causes the land surface to rise. Dissolved salts in the groundwater ultimately rise to leave a crust of white 'trona' (sodium bicarbonate) on the surface. The highly alkaline soils associated with trona are toxic to most plants except Spike Grass, and islands assume an atoll-like appearance with barren interiors. Chief's Island is probably the result of tectonic uplift.

Riverine Forest

Riverine forest is typified by tall trees with interlocking crowns and a tangled understorey dominated by shrubs and creepers. Grasses are sparse or absent. The ready availability of groundwater allows large trees to grow close together, but they must then compete for light and this results in tall trunks and relatively small crowns.

This forest type grows wherever alluvial soils occur alongside water, but are sufficiently raised to prevent waterlogging of the root zone. The banks of the upper reaches of the Okavango and Kwando rivers are densely forested for a width of up to 100 m, but the forests along the Chobe River (inside the national park) have been severely denuded by browsing African Elephant. Forest is again present along the Chobe at Kasane, and along the Zambezi in the vicinity of Katima Mulilo. Larger islands are fringed with dense forest and may be completely forested in some cases.

Typical trees are Jackalberry *Diospyros mespiliformis*, Birdplum *Berchemia discolor*, Mangosteen *Garcinia livingstonei*, Sycamore Fig *Ficus sycomorus* and Sausage Tree *Kigelia africana*. Wild Date Palm *Phoenix reclinata* often dominates the outermost fringe, while Knobthorn *Acacia nigrescens* and Rain Tree *Lonchocarpus capassa* are frequent on the landward side. Confetti Bush *Maytenus senegalensis* and Red Star Apple *Diospyros lycioides* are common understorey plants.

Among mammals, Bushbuck and Leopard are most often seen in this habitat. Fig trees attract Peters' Epauletted Fruit Bat and Green Pigeon, while Pel's Fishing Owl, Paradise Flycatcher, Redbilled Helmetshrike and Yellow White-eye occur in densely foliaged trees. Butterflies and other insects may be particularly abundant.

Savanna and Scrub

Savanna is an open, park-like habitat with trees widely spaced and a ground cover of various grass species. In their mature stage, trees are generally fire-resistant but saplings are vulnerable to fire and browsing. Mixed species thickets often occur on termite mounds protected from fire. This habitat is typical of alluvial soils with different species dominating on compact silt and looser sand.

Knobthorn Savanna (*Acacia nigrescens*) dominates on alluvial soils adjacent to floodplains, while **Umbrellathorn Savanna** (*Acacia tortilis*) dominates on shallower, less well-drained soils. Palatable grass species abound, and large herbivores may be seasonally abundant in these habitats. Elephants relish the bark of Umbrellathorn and may destroy mature trees. Typical animals are Giraffe, Blue Wildebeest, Lion, Scrub Hare, Bushveld Gerbil, Crowned Plover, Tawny Eagle, Scops Owl, Yellowbilled Hornbill and Puff Adder. **Camelthorn Savanna** (*Acacia erioloba*) is dominant in the now dry riverbed at Savuti where Kalahari sand is the substrate.

When savanna is heavily utilised by herbivores, overgrazing may result. Favourable conditions for termites ensue and grass re-growth is inhibited. Once the grass cover is denuded, fires cannot burn for lack of fuel and impenetrable *Acacia* scrub may result. Buffalothorn *Ziziphus mucronata* and Sicklebush *Dichrostachys cinerea* are also prone to form dense scrubby communities largely devoid of grass.

Mopane Scrub (*Colophospermum mopane*), characterised by low, multi-stemmed plants, is typical of shallow soil underlain with calcrete. This dense habitat – relatively unfavourable for wildlife – is typical of the eastern parts of Moremi.

Woodland

BUSTER CULVERWELL/AFRICAN IMAGES

Woodland differs from savanna in that the trees are more closely spaced, with crowns almost touching one another. Trees are deciduous, but may still carry old foliage when new growth appears in spring. Grass cover is sparser and less palatable to herbivores. Fire is less frequent, although leaf litter may act as fuel. Three woodland types are found in the region, each characteristic of a particular soil type.

Mopane Woodland (*Colophospermum mopane*) prevails over much of the area, growing on poorly drained clay soils where its shallow root system enables it to gather moisture from the upper surface. Grasses of many species occur, but are generally less palatable than savanna species. Baobab *Adansonia digitata*, Russet Bushwillow *Combretum hereroense* and Shepherd's Tree *Boscia albitrunca* often occur at the woodland margin. African Elephant are particularly fond of Mopane and cause considerable damage by stripping bark and pushing over trees. Other typical animals are Greater Kudu, Tree Squirrel, Crested Francolin, Redbilled Hornbill, Burchell's Starling, Arnot's Chat, Rock Monitor and Mopane Snake. Seasonal, rain-filled pans are a feature and may attract considerable numbers of animals.

Zambezi Teak Woodland (*Baikiaea plurijuga*) occurs on well-drained Kalahari sands. This tree is not popular with Elephant, so the woodland is taller and less battered than Mopane. Kiaat *Pterocarpus angolensis* and Wild Syringa *Burkea africana* also occur. Sable Antelope, Swallowtailed Bee-eater and Blackheaded Oriole are typical.

Silver Terminalia Woodland (*Terminalia sericea*) is typical of transition zones between clay and sand. This tree may also form pure stands on deep sand and, like Mopane, may occur as low scrub.

Rocky Outcrops

The entire northern Botswana and Caprivi region is flat or gently undulating. Only in a few places is the cover of deep Kalahari sand or alluvial silt interrupted by rocky outcrops, but these sites are so different from the surrounding landscape that they are singled out here as habitats in their own right. Tectonic uplift may have been responsible for the formation of these hills.

Best known, though remote and rarely featured on the itinerary of tourists, are the Tsodilo Hills (pictured above). Situated some 40 km south of Shakawe and west of the Okavango Delta, these Hills are famous for the magnificent outdoor gallery of San/Bushmen rock paintings – mostly depicting wildlife – which adorn the cliffs and over-hangs. Tsodilo is, in fact, a jumble of four rocky outcrops of which the highest rises about 300 m above the surrounding Kalahari sands. Standing atop these Hills provides the best (and unless you are in an aeroplane, the only) view across the Kalahari. A number of Khoisan-speaking !Kung reside in the vicinity of the Hills, but their continued presence here is the subject of some controversy. Tragically, some of the finest of these rock paintings have been defaced in recent years.

Other hills are to be found near the now dry Savuti Channel in the Chobe National Park. Much smaller than Tsodilo, but more accessible, the Gubatsaa and Gcoha hills have less impressive rock paintings but afford good views.

Typical trees are Lavender Feverberry *Croton gratissimus* and White Syringa *Kirkia acuminata*. Leopard may have lairs among the rocks. Reptiles are abundant and include African Rock Python and Rock Monitor.

Mammals

The Okavango Delta and surrounding wildlife reserves of northern Botswana support one the world's last and greatest assemblages of large, free-ranging mammals. African Elephant, Wild Dog, Red Lechwe and Tsessebe occur in greater numbers here than in almost any other part of Africa. The swamp-adapted Sitatunga is found nowhere else south of the Zambezi. Lion, Leopard and Cheetah occur in good numbers. Large mammal populations in Caprivi are recovering within the newly proclaimed reserves after having being subjected to excessive hunting in the past two decades.

Many of the larger herbivores – in particular Burchell's Zebra, Tsessebe, Buffalo and African Elephant – are prone to seasonal movements, although these are being increasingly curtailed as veterinary cordon fences are erected. In recent years, both the Black and White Rhinoceros have become extinct in the region; the latter despite an intensive reintroduction programme.

Names used follow those in the region's standard reference work – *The Mammals of the Southern African Subregion* by J. Skinner and R. Smithers (Univ. of Pretoria, 1990) – but hyphens have been deleted. Chris and Tilde Stuart's *Field Guide to the Mammals of Southern Africa* (Struik, 1988) is a more portable yet comprehensive guide book. *Field Guide to the Tracks and Signs of Southern and East African Wildlife* (Southern, 1994) – also by Chris and Tilde Stuart – is an extremely useful publication. Two excellent books on mammal behaviour are *Behaviour Guide to African Mammals* by Richard D. Estes (Russel Friedman, 1995) and *Wild Ways* by Peter Apps (Southern, 1992).

African Elephant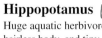

Huge herbivore. Males are larger than females, with a rounded rather than angular forehead and thicker tusks. Dominant females (matriarchs) lead family units which may combine to form herds of several hundred. Males usually keep to themselves in smaller 'bachelor' groups. Feeds on leaves, bark and grass for over 14 hours of each day and modifies woodlands in the process. Dependent on water.
Height: up to 4 m   Mass: up to 6 000 kg (male)

Hippopotamus

Huge aquatic herbivore with an almost hairless body, and tiny ears and eyes. The broad mouth has tusk-like teeth. Keeps to water by day, when only its ears, eyes and nostrils protrude above surface. Comes onto land after dark to feed on grass. Usually found in small herds of 10 to 12. Noisy and aggressive, fearsome clashes ensue between rival males. Plays a role in the maintenance and creation of channels.
Height: 1.5 m   Mass: up to 2 000 kg (male)

LEX HES

Burchell's Zebra

Horse-like herbivore which lives in family units of several mares and their offspring, and a single stallion. Grazer of tall or short grass, and often the first to feed at new growth after fire. May congregate during the rainy season to form large herds – most notably at Savuti. Each individual has a unique coat pattern. Call is a bark-like 'gwa-ha'. Lion and Spotted Hyena are the chief predators.
Height: 1.3 m Mass: up to 340 kg

Warthog

Sparsely haired pig with curved tusks and wart-like swellings on the face. Males larger with longer tusks and two pairs of 'warts'. The tail is held upright when on the run. Grazes on short grass or digs for tubers on folded knees. Partial to wallowing in mud. Strictly diurnal, retreating to burrow after dark. Sexes live apart, with females caring for piglets. Preyed upon by all larger carnivores but brave in defence.
Height: up to 70 cm Mass: up to 105 kg (male)

WILDERNESS SAFARIS/COLIN BELL

Giraffe

Massive long-necked herbivore. Feeds on leaves beyond the reach of other browsers. Favours *Acacia* during summer, but switches to Mopane and evergreen trees in the dry season. Social but non-territorial. The small horns of males are bald on their tips; those of females are tufted. Individuals become darker with age. Ageing adults and calves are vulnerable to Lion and Spotted Hyena.
Height: up to 5 m Mass: up to 1 400 kg (male)

MARK TENNANT/AFRICAN IMAGES

Buffalo

Massive relative of the domestic cow with a short, sparse coat. Gregarious but non-territorial. Family units may congregate in herds of several hundred or more during the dry season, gathering to feed on nutritious grass. Older bulls often form small groups. Keeps to shade for much of the day, feeding mostly at night. Lion are the main predators. Calves are vulnerable to Spotted Hyena but the herd affords good security and protection.
Height: 1.4 m Mass: up to 700 kg (male)

WILDERNESS SAFARIS/COLIN BELL

Red Lechwe ✓

Handsome, chestnut-coated antelope favouring edges of marshes and quick to enter water. Deeply splayed hooves allow movement in mud. The hindquarters are raised and **bold black lines run down the front of the forelegs**. Males carry lyre-shaped horns. Selective grazers of grasses and sedges. Occurs in small breeding units or in larger aggregations with numerous competing males. Lion are main predators.
Height: 1 m Horns: 70 cm Mass: 100 kg (male)

Common Waterbuck ✓

Large, robust antelope less common than might be expected in the region. The coat of long hair is grey-brown and the rump distinctively marked with a **broad white ring**. Only males possess horns. Rarely found far from water but not as aquatic as the previous species. Territorial bulls rule over groups of females. Grazes on floodplains or in open woodland. Preyed upon by all larger carnivores.
Height: 1.3 m Horns: 75 cm Mass: 260 kg (male)

Common Reedbuck

Medium-sized, reddish-brown antelope. Pairs hold territories but boundaries are not well defined. A sharp whistle is the contact and alarm call. Only males have horns. Largely nocturnal, but when active during the day keeps mostly to long grass. Told from the similar **Puku** (which is found only along Chobe River) by bushy tail and dark band down front of forelegs.
Height: 80-95 cm Horns: 30 cm Mass: 60 kg

Sable Antelope

Horse-like antelope with long mane and swept-back horns. Males are jet-black with contrasting white facial pattern and underbelly; younger females chestnut with shorter and thinner horns. Selective grazer, but will also browse on occasion. Female herds of 10 to 25 range over an area incorporating territory of dominant bull. May fall prey to Lion, but attacked with caution.
Height: 1.3 m Horns: 1 m Mass: 180-270 kg
ss: Roan Antelope (grey, larger, shorter horns)

Sitatunga

Elusive, aquatic antelope confined to papyrus swamp and adjacent land. Males have shaggy, plain brown coats, while females are reddish with white stripes on the flanks and spots on the rump. Males have spiral horns. Feeds on aquatic vegetation as well as on grass and leaves. Uses regular pathways through papyrus. A good but slow swimmer. Lion and Wild Dog are the main predators.

Height: 90 cm Horns: 60 cm Mass: 115 kg (male)

LEX HES

Bushbuck

Primarily nocturnal, this shy antelope may also be active at dusk and dawn. Browses on leaves but also feeds on grass, fruit and flowers. The sub-species found in this area is more colourful than those to the south, its rich red coat lined with up to eight white stripes and numerous white spots. Only the male carries horns. Most frequent along the Chobe River. Leopard is the main predator.

Height: 75 cm Horns: 26 cm Mass: 45 kg (male)

C & T STUART

Greater Kudu

Large browsing antelope favouring dry woodland. Males carry magnificent spiral horns which attain full length after three years. The coat is grey-brown with six or more thin white stripes. Males have a prominent mane on the shoulders and throat. Females gather in small herds, with males in tow during midwinter rut. Non-breeding males form bachelor herds. Lion is the main predator.

Height: 1.5 m Horns: 1.2 m Mass: 250 kg (male)

Impala

Graceful reddish antelope favouring edges of woodland. Tuft of black hair on ankle of hind leg is diagnostic. Males have lyre-shaped horns. Adaptable grazer-browser. Herds of females occupy a home range, and males establish territories during the rut (peak in April-May) with much roaring, snorting and chasing of rivals. Non-breeding males form bachelor herds. Lambs are born in spring. Wild Dog and Cheetah are among the predators.

Height: 90 cm Horns: 50 cm Mass: 50 kg (male)

PETER HANCOCK

Tsessebe

Large antelope with a distinctive **sloping back**. Short coat is reddish-brown with maroon sheen and with darker head and upper legs. Both sexes carry short, ringed horns. Small herds of females occupy a home range which overlaps territory of male. Large herds gather in Savuti at the end of summer. Selective grazer of low grasses. Said to be the fastest of all antelope. Preyed upon by Lion.

Height: 1.2 m Horns: 34 cm Mass: 140 kg (male)

Blue Wildebeest

Large antelope with weak hindquarters and strong forequarters. Adults are grey with a black face and mane and darker creases on sides. Both sexes have horns. Young are tawny coated. Bulls territorial during breeding season. Gregarious, favouring open country. Bulk grazer of short grass. Lion and Spotted Hyena are the main predators. Mass migrations now reduced, but seasonal movements occur.

Height: 1.5 m Horns: 60 cm Mass: 250 kg (male)

Steenbok

Small, brick-red antelope with **large rounded ears**. Only males have horns. Prefers drier open areas with thickets for cover. Mixed feeder of grass, leaves, seed pods and berries. Independent of drinking water. Monogamous and usually seen in pairs. Active at all hours, but rests in shade at midday. Young born at any time of the year. Cheetah and Martial Eagle are among the predators.

Height: 50 cm Horns: 9 cm Mass: 11 kg

LEX HES

Common Duiker

Small, grey-brown antelope with heavy build. The **black blaze on the forehead and snout**, and crest of hair on the top of the head are diagnostic. Only the males have horns. Browses on a variety of shrubs and herbs, and may even feed on carrion. Most active at dusk and dawn, and also into the night. Occurs singly or in pairs in a fixed home range in well-wooded habitat. Leopard is the main predator.

Height: 50 cm Horns: 11 cm Mass: 18 kg (male)

Lion

Very large sociable cat living in prides of several adult females (often related) and their offspring, and up to three adult males. All defend a territory against rivals. Preys on anything from young Elephant to rodents, but most partial to Buffalo, Zebra and larger antelope. Also pirates kills from other carnivores, and scavenges. Most active at night. The impressive 'roar' may carry for several kilometres.
Height: 1.2 m Length: 2 to 3 m Mass: 220 kg (male)

Leopard

Large cat with relatively **short legs** and **rosettes of black spots** on tawny coat. Sexes only come together to mate. One or two cubs remain with mother for up to two years. Females have overlapping home ranges; males have larger ranges incorporating those of several females. Elusive and mostly nocturnal. Diverse diet, but small and medium-sized antelope dominate. Kills are stored in trees.
Height: 75 cm Length: 1.8 m Mass: up to 90 kg

Cheetah

Large elegant cat with **long legs**, grey-hound-like frame, **solid black spots** and black 'tear-marks' between eyes and mouth. Adult females often accompanied by two to five cubs for up to two years. Males frequently form coalitions (often brothers) of two or three. Hunts by day (mostly Impala), thereby reducing competition with other predators. Able to sprint at 112 km/h over short distances.
Height: 80 cm Length: 1.8 to 2 m Mass: 50 kg

MARK TENNANT/AFRICAN IMAGES

Serval

Medium-sized, long-legged cat with **short tail**, black **spots merging into bands**, and white bars on the back of the large ears. Males and females live apart in overlapping ranges. Usually found near water where the Angoni Vlei Rat and other rodents make up the bulk of its diet; ground birds, frogs and fish are also taken. Primarily nocturnal, elusive and shy.
Height: 60 cm Length: 1 m Mass: up to 18 kg

LEX HES

Spotted Hyena

Large, heavily built carnivore with **sloping back**. The coat is fawn with dark blotches becoming fainter with age; young pups are charcoal. Mostly nocturnal. Lives in clans of varying size with larger females dominating males; one female – the matriarch – ranks highest. Clan teams up against rivals, and hunts together (mostly Blue Wildebeest) but members clash over food. Regular scavenger. Very vocal.
Height: 85 cm Length: 1.2 to 1.8 m Mass: 70 kg

Wild Dog

Slender, long-legged carnivore with large **rounded ears** and **straight back**. Coat is dappled in dark brown, fawn and white. Sociable, it forms packs of between 6 and 15 adults (plus young-sters) with one dominant pair. Active by day, running down prey (mostly Impala and young of larger antelope) after a chase. Northern Botswana is one of the strongholds of this endangered species.
Height: 75 cm Length: 1.2 m Mass: 20 to 30 kg

Sidestriped Jackal

Greyish jackal with **white-tipped tail** and white stripe on flanks varying in width and boldness. The snout is rather blunt and the ears shorter than those of the next species. Occurs in pairs and family groups of up to six. Usually nocturnal, favouring well-wooded areas and floodplains. Opportunistic predator of a wide variety of smaller animals and also scavenges. Call is an owl-like hoot.
Height: 40 cm Length: 1 m Mass: 8 to 12 kg

Blackbacked Jackal

Reddish-yellow jackal with pointed snout and ears, and distinctive black and silver 'saddle'. Pair defends territory and raises three to four pups which remain with parents to help feed next litter. Numbers may congregate to scavenge from large carcasses. Prey ranges from insects to young Impala, as well as berries. Favours drier, more open areas than the previous species. Call is a drawn-out wail.
Height: 38 cm Length: 1 m Mass: 6 to 10 kg

Bateared Fox

Small, bushy-tailed fox with enormous ears, grizzled grey coat and short black legs. The face is masked in black and the forehead is white. Favours drier open areas with short grass. Most active at twilight and after dark, but frequently about by day during winter. Lives in groups of three to seven consisting of a monogamous pair and their offspring. Feeds on termites and other small prey.
Height: 35 cm Length: 80 cm Mass: 4 kg

Honey Badger (Ratel)

Stout, short-legged carnivore boldly marked in black and silvery-white. Usually seen alone, but likely to live in monogamous pairs. A powerful and avid digger, it uses its strong claws to unearth mole rats and other prey. Climbs trees for honey and bee larvae, but relationship with Greater Honeyguide is contentious. Strips bark off trees in search of reptiles. May enter camps to scavenge.
Height: 30 cm Length: 1 m Mass: 8 to 14 kg

MARK TENNANT/AFRICAN IMAGES

Civet

Robust, raccoon-like carnivore with a distinctive **black mask**, boldly marked coat and ringed tail. Long spinal crest is raised when alarmed. Nocturnal, but may be seen prowling sand roads and open areas after dark. Diet is diverse and includes millipedes, snakes and the fruit of the Wild Date Palm. Solitary and territorial. Scent-marks frequently and creates specific latrine sites.
Height: 40 cm Length: 1.2 m Mass: 9 to15 kg

C & T STUART

Largespotted Genet

Slim, short-legged carnivore with spotted coat and long ringed tail, usually **black tipped**. Spots vary in colour from black to rusty. Strictly nocturnal and most often seen in branches of trees or running across roads. Solitary and territorial. Preys on a wide variety of creatures from insects to nestling birds. The similar **Smallspotted Genet** differs in having a **white-tipped tail** and pure black spots.
Height: 45 cm Length: 1 m Mass: 2 to 3 kg

LEX HES

Banded Mongoose

Stocky mongoose with distinctive vertical bars on back and flanks of grizzled coat. Gregarious, living in troops of up to 35 with up to four breeding females and males. Active by day within a defined home range. Packs move together but individuals forage separately and guard food jealously. Invertebrates, small reptiles and birds' eggs are favoured. Den is in a termite mound within a thicket.
Length: 55 cm Mass: 1 to 1.5 kg

Dwarf Mongoose

Tiny mongoose with glossy reddish coat. Lives in troops of about ten (but up to 30) with a single breeding pair. Active by day within a defined home range. Pack moves together but individuals pursue invertebrate prey independently. Den is often in an exposed termite mound. At first glance it could be confused with **Tree Squirrel** (opposite). **Slender Mongoose** is larger, solitary and has a dark tip to its long tail.
Length: 35 cm Mass: 220 to 350 g

Water (Marsh) Mongoose

Large, **shaggy-coated** mongoose found in the vicinity of water. Dark colour and semi-aquatic habits may lead to confusion with two otter species (but both have short coats). Occurs singly or in pairs, using regular pathways and latrine sites within a linear territory. Feeds on frogs, crabs, fish and invertebrates caught mostly in shallow water. Active mainly at night but may be seen at dusk.
Length: up to 1 m Height: 22 cm Mass: 3 to 5 kg

Cape Clawless Otter

Large, low-slung carnivore with short coat of dark brown fur. Underbelly and throat are plain white. Always found in or around water where it hunts for crabs, fish and frogs. Streamlined tail acts as a rudder and paddle. Front feet are **unwebbed** and distinctive spoor shows no claw-marks. The smaller **Spottednecked Otter** has **webbed toes** and is more aquatic (rarely leaving water).
Length: 1 to 1.5 m Mass: 10 to 18 kg
ss: Spottednecked Otter (Mass: 3 to 5 kg)

Tree Squirrel

Small, bushy-tailed rodent with grey to yellow-brown coat, paler underneath. Keeps mostly to trees but runs nimbly on the ground. Most abundant in mature Mopane woodland, but occurs in most habitats. Usually seen singly or in small family group. Males may be territorial. A chattering, bird-like call is made in alarm and often indicates the presence of an eagle, snake or other predator.

Length: 35 cm Mass: 100 to 250 g

Lesser Bushbaby (Night Ape)

Tiny nocturnal primate with huge bulging eyes and long fluffy tail. Bounds through trees with great agility. Female and offspring occupy a home range; males have larger territories incorporating ranges of several females. Aerial pathways are scent-marked with urine. Family groups sleep together in day nest. Feeds on insects and resin of acacia trees. Calls include a high-pitched wail. Restless.

Length: 35 cm (incl. 20 cm tail) Mass: 150 g

LEX HES

Vervet Monkey

Inquisitive, agile primate with grizzled grey coat, distinctive black face and a long tail. Lives in troops of up to 20, comprised of adult females and offspring, and accompanied by one or more mature males. A strict hierarchy exists between females. Readily comes to ground but retreats to trees, and sleeps on branches at night. Feeds on a variety of fruit and small animals. Often enters camps.

Length: 1 to 1.3 m Mass: 4 to 5 kg

IAN SUTHERLAND/AFRICAN IMAGES

Chacma Baboon

Large, dog-like primate with shaggy, grey-brown coat and long bare snout. Males much larger than females, which have naked buttocks able to change in colour and shape depending upon sexual condition. Babies often ride on mother's back. Lives in troops of up to 100, with adult males in strict hierarchy. Feeds on a wide variety of plants and animals. Often associates with Impala. Very vocal.

Length: up to 1.6 m (male) Mass: 32 kg (male)

Scrub Hare

The **long ears**, **short bushy tail** and **grizzled grey coat** prevent confusion with the next species. Nocturnal in habits but may be flushed from resting place during the day; sometimes active in the late afternoon or early morning. Runs in a typical zig-zag fashion when disturbed. Feeds primarily on grass. Raises litters of one to three each year. Predators include Giant Eagle Owl, Serval and Leopard.
Length: 53 cm Mass: 2 to 4 kg

LEX HES

Springhare

Unusual, kangaroo-like rodent with large eyes and squared-off snout. Hops on powerful hind legs, using front limbs only for digging and holding food. The **coat is fawn-coloured**, and the long bushy tail tipped in black. Occurs in colonies in open areas of compressed sandy soil. Strictly nocturnal, staying in underground burrows during the day, and rarely straying far from them when grazing at night.
Length: 80 cm Mass: 2 to 3.5 kg

C & T STUART

Angoni Vlei Rat

Short-tailed rodent with a blunt nose, shaggy fur and round ears. Occurs in dense vegetation near water. Active during both night and day, making use of runs and tunnels in order to reach feeding sites. Grass roots, reeds and sedges are favoured. Preyed upon by Serval and various raptors. Although only visible when skulls are examined, the upper incisors are deeply grooved.
Length: 30 cm (incl. 8 cm tail) Mass: 100 to 250 g

C & T STUART

Greater Cane Rat

Large, beaver-like rodent with coarse grizzled coat. The head is small in relation to the body, and the ears are tiny. The short tail is almost naked. Lives in small colonies in reedbeds, feeding on stems and roots of sedges, reeds and grasses. Regular pathways are used. Nocturnal, but sometimes active at dusk. Predators include Rock Python and Leopard.
Length: 65 to 80 cm Mass: 3 to 5 kg

Tree Mouse

Small rodent with **long black tail**. Lives exclusively in trees where its **twig nests** are conspicuous; the Camelthorn and other acacias are favoured. May also live in tree holes. The upperparts are grey-fawn and the underparts pure white. Lives in family groups. Nocturnal, but often emerges at dusk and may be seen scurrying along branches. Feeds on seeds, seed-pods and small insects.

Length: 30 cm (incl. 15 cm tail) Mass: 100 g

Woodland Dormouse

Small, silvery-grey rodent with white underparts and **bushy, squirrel-like tail**. It is at home in the branches of trees (especially acacias) and may also frequent structures around homesteads. Strictly nocturnal, its diet includes insects, spiders and seeds. A substantial **nest of fine grass**, lichen and leaves is constructed within a tree hole or similar cavity.

Length: 16 cm (incl. 7 cm tail) Mass: 30 g

NATIONAL PARKS BOARD OF S.A.

Singlestriped Mouse

Small rodent with upperparts varying in colour from grey to fawn. The **single dark stripe** running down the centre of the back is diagnostic. Diurnal, and therefore the most frequently seen rodent. Spends all its time on the ground and is often seen running across tracks and at roadsides. Grass seeds are the main food, and numbers fluctuate in relation to rainfall. Preyed upon by smaller raptors.

Length: 27 cm (incl. 15 cm tail) Mass: 60 g

NATIONAL PARKS BOARD OF S.A.

Bushveld Gerbil

Reddish-brown rodent with pure white underparts and diagnostic dark stripe running down the length of its sparsely haired tail. Nocturnal, living in small colonies. Most common in areas of sandy soil where burrows are excavated. Feeds on seeds and insects. As with other gerbils, this species is a vector for the plague virus, but it rarely lives near man so contact with fleas is rare.

Length: 28 cm (incl. 15 cm tail) Mass: 70 g
ss: Highveld Gerbil (no stripe down tail)

C & T STUART

LEX HES

Porcupine

Large nocturnal rodent with long black and white quills. Vegetarian, it is an avid digger, feeding primarily on roots and tubers. Tree bark is also favoured. Days are spent in a burrow. Its presence may be detected by gnaw marks on tree trunks and discarded quills. The quills may be raised in alarm, and are used in defence against predators such as Leopard and Lion.

Length: 75 to 100 cm Mass: 10 to 24 kg

C & T STUART

Shortsnouted Elephant Shrew

Small insectivore which – despite its name – has a long snout (albeit shorter than that of other elephant shrews). The reddish-yellow coat is flecked with black, the underbelly and throat are white, and the large eyes are ringed in white or buff. Keeps to well-wooded areas with longer grass, including Mopane scrub. Diurnal, but most active at dawn.

Length: 21 cm (incl. 10 cm tail) Mass: 44 g
ss: Bushveld Elephant Shrew (dry open areas)

NATIONAL PARKS BOARD OF S.A.

Lesser Red Musk Shrew

Tiny nocturnal insectivore with pointed snout and small rounded ears. A voracious predator of small insects and worms, often eating the equivalent of its own body weight each night. May be seen in camps where it feeds on insects drawn to light. Males engage in fierce fights, squealing loudly in the process. Young clasp mother's tail when on the move.

Length: 13 cm (incl. 5 cm tail) Mass: 16 g
ss: Swamp Musk Shrew; Giant Musk Shrew

Peters' Epauletted Fruit Bat

Large, fruit-eating bat. Males call with a resounding 'ping' – a characteristic night sound in the region. The coat is grey-yellow with **two pairs of distinctive white spots in front of, and behind, the ears**. Males have tufts of white hair on the shoulders which are erected into 'epaulettes' during display. Roosts within dense foliage or under thatch. Navigates by sight. Figs are the favoured food.

Length: 15 cm Wingspan: 56 cm Mass: 100 g
ss: Strawcoloured Fruit Bat (19 cm)

Cape Serotine Bat

Tiny bat frequently seen flying at dusk in the company of swallows and swifts. Small airborne insects such as mosquitoes and moths are the quarry, and are hunted well into the night. By day, they roost in tree holes, among palm fronds or under roofs. Pale brown above and off-white below. The snout is pointed and the ears are short.

Length: 8 cm Wingspan: 23 cm Mass: 6 g
ss: Somali Serotine Bat (8 cm, 5 g)

Common Slitfaced Bat

Small bat characterised by a longitudinal slit running down the face (this, however, is difficult to see). The wings are rounded and the tail is broad with a notched tip. The most obvious feature is, however, the **long and conspicuous ears**. Roosts in colonies of several hundred in caves or man-made structures, or holes in Baobab trees. Rarely emerges until well after dark.

Length: 10 cm   Wingspan: 24 cm Mass: 11 g

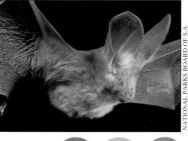

Yellow House Bat

Stoutly built, insectivorous bat with short ears and pointed snout. Roosts in small groups under branches or the eaves of buildings. Emerges after dark to feed on flying insects, often around outdoor lights. True to its name, this species has a distinctive yellow belly, with darker upperparts. The membranous tail ends in an acute point.

Length: 13 cm Wingspan: 30 cm Mass: 27 g
ss: Lesser Yellow House Bat (12 cm, 16 g)

Little Freetailed Bat

Tiny insectivorous bat occurring in a wide variety of habitats. Uniform brown to sandy-fawn in colour, with large ears and a wrinkled, mastiff-like face. The distinctive feature is the small thin tail which protrudes beyond the tail membrane. Gregarious, it roosts by day in tree holes, palm fronds, roofs or other man-made structures.

Length: 9 cm Wingspan: 24 cm Mass: 11 g
ss: Egyptian Freetailed Bat (11 cm, 15 g)

Birds

Over 500 bird species have been recorded in the Okavango Delta, Chobe and Caprivi region, making this one of the finest birdwatching localities on the continent. In this section 198 of the more common or interesting birds – including Pel's Fishing Owl, Copperytailed Coucal, Lesser Jacana, African Skimmer and Slaty Egret – are featured. Due to limitations of space, some species which may be fairly common in Caprivi have been excluded in favour of birds likely to be seen in the Okavango.

More bird species occur during the summer months, when migrants from further afield are present, and when smaller songbirds are most vocal. In winter, however, the sparser vegetation is an advantage when looking for bush birds, and waterfowl tend to congregate in larger numbers. Most of the 'specials' are present throughout the year. Campsites and lodges, where you are able to walk about, are excellent places to look for smaller birds. When driving, the most useful tip is to stop and turn the car motor off at regular intervals – this will allow you to hear birds calling, and see movement in trees.

The species are arranged in such a way that those which could be confused appear on the same spread, and this has resulted in a slightly different sequence from that of the standard reference works. The names used are those recognised by the South African Ornithological Society. The two most comprehenisive field guides are *Birds of Botswana* by Kenneth Newman (Southern, 1989) and *Sasol Birds of Southern Africa* (Struik, 1993). Huw Penry's *Bird Atlas of Botswana* (Natal University Press, 1994) provides information on distribution and status.

MARK TENNANT/AFRICAN IMAGES

Ostrich

Huge flightless bird with long neck and legs. Males are predominantly black with white wings and ginger tail plumes; when breeding the pink scales on the shins become red. Females are dull grey-brown. Occurs in pairs when breeding, but thereafter in small flocks. Often associates with antelope. Wary, and able to run at great speeds. Most common in more open areas such as Savuti.
Height: 2 m

Dabchick (Little Grebe)

Small waterbird, superficially resembling a duck. The **chestnut neck and pale spot at the base of the bill** – of breeding adults – are diagnostic, as is the habit of diving below the surface of the water to catch small fish, crabs and frogs. May be found on any stretch of water, but favours pans. A loud trill is the call, often uttered during courtship.
Length: 20 cm

Reed Cormorant

Medium-sized, black waterbird with a long tail and **red eyes**. Immature birds have an off-white breast. In common with other cormorants, the feathers are not waterproof and it regularly perches with its wings outstretched so that they may dry. Fish are caught underwater. Breeds colonially in large trees or in reedbeds, often in the company of herons or storks.

Length: 52 cm   ss: Whitebreasted Cormorant

African Darter

Large, dark brown waterbird with a long neck – often held in an S-bend shape – and a sharp, pointed bill. Breeding adults have a rufous throat edged in white. The wings are held outstretched to dry. Dives for fish, which are speared before being brought to the surface. Often swims with only the neck and head above water, leading to its alternative name of Snakebird.

Length: 80 cm

Eastern White Pelican

Massive white bird with long neck, short legs. The bare skin around the eye and the upper bill is pink, the lower bill and pouch bright yellow. In flight, the **black flight feathers** are conspicuous. Fish are the primary food. Gregarious. Breeds in colonies on the bare ground of salt pans. Nomadic. The smaller **Pinkbacked Pelican** has grey flight feathers.

Length: 1.8 m ss: Pinkbacked Pelican (1.4 m, grey-white plumage, pale pinkish-yellow bill)

African Spoonbill

Large, all-white waterbird with distinctive, spoon-shaped bill. The long legs and bare face of adults are pink. Flies with neck outstretched. The bill is used in a sweeping motion in shallow water to capture small crustaceans and aquatic insects; small fish and frogs may also be taken. Occurs singly or in flocks which fly in V-formation. Often nests alongside other species in reedbeds or dead trees.

Length: 90 cm

Goliath Heron

Massive, slate-grey heron with rufous head, neck and underparts. The immature is paler with white throat extending to the chest. Usually nests among reeds away from other species. Occurs singly or in pairs, often standing motionless at water's edge. Large fish and crabs are the main food but baby crocodiles may also be taken. Flies with slow, deep wingbeats; the neck is tucked in.
Length: 1.4 m

Purple Heron

Slender rufous heron with a **grey crown** and **boldly striped face and neck**. The immature has a chestnut back, unstriped face and off-white belly. Usually seen alone or in the company of other wading birds. Numbers may gather at evening roosts and it often breeds colonially. Feeds on fish, frogs and large insects. If disturbed it often assumes a rigid, upright stance among reeds.
Length: 90 cm

Grey Heron

Large, pale grey heron with **white head and neck**, and long yellow bill. A bold black streak runs above and behind the eye to form a small crest. In flight, the **underwing is uniform grey**. Usually seen alone on floodplains or the verges of rivers and lagoons where it hunts for frogs and fish. The nest is a platform of reeds and sticks, built in a tree or reedbed.
Length: 100 cm ss: Blackheaded Heron (under-wing grey and black, forages mostly on dry land)

Blackcrowned Night Heron

Small, short-necked heron. The face and underparts are snow-white, and contrast sharply with the black crown and mantle. The wings are slate-grey, and the **eyes are bright red**. Young birds are brown on the back with white spots. Nocturnal, but may be seen flying from roosts at dusk. Groups roost in dense trees or reedbeds by day. Feeds on frogs, nestling birds and insects.
Length: 56 cm ss: Whitebacked Night Heron

JOHN CARLYON

36

Great White Egret

Large, all-white egret with long neck. The **legs and toes are black at all times**. Prior to breeding, the bill is black and the bare skin around eyes lime-green. The bill and bare skin is yellow during and after breeding. Favours floodplains where it usually occurs singly, or in the company of other species. Feeds on fish, frogs and rodents. A stick nest is built within reedbeds or on the branches of a dead tree.

Length: 75 cm ss: Yellowbilled Egret (66 cm)

Little Egret

Small, all-white egret with long neck. The **yellow toes at the ends of dark legs** are diagnostic. Fine white plumes droop from the back of the head and mantle during the breeding season. The bill is black at all times. Occurs in and around water, often as the only member of its species among other herons and storks. Feeds on small fish, frogs and insects. Nests colonially with other species.

Length: 65 cm ss: Yellowbilled Egret (black toes)

Cattle Egret

Small, all-white egret with relatively short neck. When breeding, the crown, mantle and chest are adorned in buffy plumes, the bill and legs are coral-pink and the toes black. Non-breeding birds have a yellow bill and olive-brown legs and toes. Gregarious, feeding on dry land in the company of large mammals which disturb insect prey. Roosts and breeds in reedbeds or trees.

Length: 54 cm ss: Yellowbilled Egret (66 cm)

Squacco Heron

Small squat heron. Buffy in colour when seen foraging or at rest, but shows broad **white wings and tail in flight**. Breeding birds have a turquoise bill with black tip. Immatures are darker on the back and streaky below. Usually seen alone, skulking in vegetated fringes of channels and lagoons, or on floodplains. Feeds on frogs and aquatic insects. Nests colonially, often with other species.

Length: 45 cm ss: Little Bittern (26 cm)

Greenbacked Heron

Small dark heron, with short neck and yellow-green legs. The back is dark grey-green with buffy edges to wing feathers, the crown black, and the underside blue-grey. Immature birds are streaked on the throat and face, and spotted with white on the wings. Often draws attention to itself by the harsh croaking call, uttered in flight. Readily perches on exposed branches. Forages at water's edge.

Length: 40 cm ss: Dwarf Bittern (25 cm)

Rufousbellied Heron

Small, blue-black heron with **rufous belly, wings and tail**. The legs, lower bill and bare facial skin are pale yellow. Rather secretive and prefers to forage among tall vegetation. Usually seen when flushed from floodplains or along channels. Breeds colonially, usually among the branches of the Water Fig and often in the company of other species. Feeds on frogs, molluscs, fish and insects.

Length: 58 cm

Slaty Egret

Slender, slate-grey egret with **chestnut throat** (not always obvious), **yellow-green legs** and **pale eyes** distinguishing it from the next species. Usually seen alone or among other wading birds on floodplains or at the edge of channels and rivers. Wades in shallow water, shuffling feet to disturb prey in silt and mud. Roosts and nests in small groups in reedbeds. Largely confined to Okavango region.

Length: 60 cm

Black Egret

Slender, all-black egret with **dark legs, yellow toes** and **dark eyes**. The feeding behaviour is unique and diagnostic, with the wings being arched over the back to form an umbrella-like dome. This reduces glare on the surface of the water and may also attract fish into what they believe to be a shady retreat. Usually seen alone or in company of other wading birds. Breeds in reedbeds.

Length: 66 cm

Hamerkop

Plain brown bird with distinctive, back-ward-pointing crest and pointed bill giving the head a hammer-like shape. Occurs singly or in pairs. Often spends long periods standing motionless at the water's edge, waiting for opportunities to catch frogs and other aquatic life. A huge, dome-shaped nest of twigs and mud is built in the fork of a large tree. The call is a squeaky 'kiepp'.
Length: 55 cm

Hadeda Ibis

Heavy-bodied, short-legged ibis, and one of the noisiest of birds. The plumage is predominantly olive-green, but a metallic sheen of purple and emerald is present on the shoulders. Forages most often beneath shady trees where insects and worms are extracted from the soil or among leaves. Groups fly to and from tree-top roosts at dawn and dusk. A stick nest is built within the canopy of a tree.
Length: 75 cm

Glossy Ibis

Slender, chocolate-brown ibis with long legs. During the summer breeding season, the plumage becomes glossy and bronzed. Always found near water, where it occurs singly or in flocks. It wades in the shallows in search of frogs, crustaceans and aquatic insects. Small platform nests are made in reedbeds. Flocks fly in V-formations to and from roosts.
Length: 70 cm

Sacred Ibis

Slender white ibis with long legs and long, scythe-shaped bill. The naked black head and neck are diagnostic. Breeding adults have the tail adorned with black plumes. The flight feathers are tipped in black. The name refers to its place in Egyptian mythology. Occurs in small flocks which forage in shallow water for insects and frogs. Breeds in reedbeds or trees. Flocks fly in V-formation.
Length: 90 cm

Marabou Stork

Massive grey stork with white under-parts, enormous bill and naked head and neck. The pink face is sparsely covered with bristles. A sausage-shaped pouch hangs beneath the throat. The legs are grey, but often washed white with excreta. Feeds on carrion and attracted in large numbers to fish stranded in shrinking pools. Nests in colonies, often in Water Fig thickets. Flies with neck tucked in.
Length: 1.5 m

S **FG** **PS**

Saddlebilled Stork

Huge stork with pied plumage, and black legs with pink toes and 'knee' joints. The massive red bill is divided by a black bar and has a yellow, saddle-shaped shield on top. Males differ from females in having black (not yellow) eyes and a small yellow wattle at the base of the bill. Immature lacks any red on bill or legs. Feeds in shallow water, in pairs or family groups. Stick nest is built on a tree-top.
Length: 1.4 m

FG **PS**

Yellowbilled Stork

Large white stork with black flight feathers and red legs. Told from the next species by its slightly down-curved **yellow bill**, bare **red face** and **black tail**. When breeding, the mantle and wings are washed with pink. The immature is dull grey-white with yellowish legs and bill. Feeds in shallow water, taking frogs and insects. Nests colonially, often in Water Fig thickets on lagoon fringes.
Length: 1 m

FG **PS**

White Stork

Large white stork with black flight feathers and red legs. Told from the previous species by its straight **red bill**, white face and **white tail**. Like most other storks, the legs may be washed white with excreta. Gathers in flocks – often in the company of Abdim's Stork – to feed on grasshoppers on dry land. Often soars in thermals. Non-breeding **summer migrant** from Europe.
Length: 1.2 m

S

Woollynecked Stork

Chocolate-brown stork with faint purple iridescence on wings and **white neck** of curly feathers. A black mask surrounds the red eye and the black bill is tipped in red. Immature is duller with a pale bill and black crown. Usually found in small numbers in shallow water but large flocks may gather to feed at grasshopper swarms and bush fires. Nest is a stick bowl placed at the top of a tall tree.
Length: 85 cm

LEX HES

S FG

Openbilled Stork

Dark, grey-black stork with maroon wing feathers and breast. The characteristic gap near the tip of the pale bill allows it to be used like tweezers to extract fresh-water mussels and snails from their shells. Immatures are duller and lack any opening in the bill. Often forages alone or in small groups, but gregarious at roosts and breeding colonies in trees. Large flocks may be seen in flight at dusk.
Length: 95 cm

WILDERNESS SAFARIS/COLIN BELL

FG PS

Abdim's (Whitebellied) Stork

Small, black and white stork with purplish sheen to neck, mantle and wing coverts. The legs are pale mauve with pink toes and 'knee' joints; the bill is ochre. Blue and red skin encircles the dark eye. Gregarious, large flocks gather in short grassland to feed on grasshoppers and other insects. Often soars in thermals during the day. Nomadic, non-breeding **summer migrant** from tropical Africa.
Length: 75 cm ss: Black Stork (120 cm)

S

Wattled Crane

Huge, long-legged bird with stork-like appearance. The grey cap, bare red skin at base of bill and hanging wattles below the throat are diagnostic. Occurs in pairs or family groups of three or four. Pairs hold large territories, nesting in shallow water among reeds and performing courtship dances. Non-breeding birds may form flocks of several hundred. Feeds on tubers, molluscs and frogs.
Length: 1.2 m

WILDERNESS SAFARIS/COLIN BELL

PS FG

Pygmy Goose

Tiny, toy-like duck with green back, ochre underparts and yellow bill. Males have a white face, green cap and 'ear patches' ringed in black. Females have dark smudges on a white face. Occurs in pairs or family groups on still waters with waterlilies – the seeds of which make up the bulk of their diet. Flies rapidly, showing white wing bars. Nests in a tree hole, sometimes far from water.
Length: 33 cm

Knobbilled Duck

Large white duck with iridescent blue-green back and speckled face. The male is larger with a distinctive fleshy protuberance on the top of its bill which becomes enlarged during the breeding season. Nomadic and gregarious, flocks gather on floodplains and on the fringes of rivers and pans. Perches conspicuously on the branches of dead trees. Nests in a large tree hole.
Length: 75 cm

LEX HES

Spurwinged Goose

Massive, greenish-black goose with a variable amount of white on the face and underside. Bill and legs are pink. Males are considerably larger than females, with bare red facial skin extending beyond the eyes. Usually occurs in flocks which spend the day loafing on mudflats or in shallow water, and fly off to feeding grounds in the evening. Grass and tubers comprise the diet. Nests among reeds.
Length: 1 m

Egyptian Goose

Large, chestnut and fawn goose with a dark mask around the eyes. In flight, the black and white wings with emerald-green panels are diagnostic. Occurs in pairs or small groups on floodplains and pans, but may congregate in large flocks. Feeds mostly on grass on dry land after dark. Noisy and aggressive during the breeding season. Breeds in a large tree hole or in a Hamerkop nest.
Length: 70 cm

Whitebacked Duck

Small duck with speckled brown plumage and diagnostic **white spot at the base of the dark bill**. The white back is visible only in flight; seldom takes to the air by day. Sits low in the water with humped back, and dives below the surface to feed on seeds and tubers. May remain motionless if disturbed. Occurs in pairs or small groups on lagoons and temporary, rain-filled pans. Nests among reeds.
Length: 43 cm

Whitefaced Duck

Long-necked duck with an upright stance. It often draws attention to itself with its flute-like call. The distinctive white face, chestnut neck, and black and white barred flanks are diagnostic. May gather in flocks of several hundred at pans and rivers, spending much of its time resting at the water's edge. Feeds on aquatic tubers and seeds. A nest bowl is made among grass, often far from water.
Length: 48 cm ss: Fulvous Duck

Redbilled Teal

Small duck with diagnostic **crimson-red bill** and **dark cap**. Common, but rather inconspicuous due to its habit of foraging among vegetation. Often assembles in huge flocks (half a million were once estimated at Lake Ngami). Prefers shallow water, and is usually the first to arrive at flooded grasslands after rain. Food consists of grass seeds, grain and small aquatic creatures. Nests in grass.
Length: 48 cm   ss: Hottentot Teal (blue bill)

Yellowbilled Duck

Medium-sized duck with bright **yellow bill with a black 'saddle'**. The brown feathers are rimmed with buff, giving a spangled appearance. In flight, the turquoise wing bar edged in white is distinctive. Occurs in pairs or flocks on floodplains and in pans and along rivers. Grazes on short grass, often after dark. The nest is a grass bowl hidden among reeds.
Length: 57 cm

43

African Jacana

Slender, rust-red bird with white face and neck, and **pale blue shield of bare skin on the forehead**. Extremely long toes enable it to walk on floating vegetation and waterlily leaves. The immature has a white eye-stripe and white underparts and could be confused with the next species. Found on water bodies with emergent vegetation. Feeds on aquatic insects. Occurs singly or in small noisy groups.
Length: 28 cm

Lesser Jacana

Small jacana, about half the size of the previous species. The underparts are white, the crown chestnut and sides of the neck buffy yellow. A white eye-stripe is distinctive, and the **white tips to the flight feathers** (visible in flight) are diagnostic. May occur alongside its larger relative but is much less conspicuous. Feeds on aquatic insects. Occurs in pairs or family groups.
Length: 15 cm

Black Crake

Small, jet-black bird with **lime-yellow bill and bright red legs**. Inconspicuous and shy but much less so than other crakes. Often located by its call – a harsh throaty warble, frequently a duet between a pair. The very long toes allow it to run across floating vegetation. Small aquatic insects are the main food. The nest is well-hidden amongst reeds or papyrus.
Length: 21 cm ss: African Crake

Purple Gallinule

Sizeable, chicken-sized bird with purple and turquoise underparts, and olive back. The stout bill and frontal shield are coral-pink. Occurs singly or in pairs in dense swampy habitats, but is secretive. Most often seen in the dry season when it occasionally strides out from cover on its long pink legs into shallow water. Feeds on tubers, sedge stems and nestling birds.
Length: 45 cm

Wood Sandpiper

Small, grey-brown wader with fairly long yellow legs and a thin bill. The **dark back is boldly spotted in white** and the white eye-stripe extends to the back of the head. Common **summer migrant** usually found on mudflats and in shallow water. Many individuals may forage around a single body of water, but they tend to space themselves out. In flight, the **white rump** is conspicuous.

Length: 20 cm ss: Marsh Sandpiper (23 cm)

Common Sandpiper

Small, grey-brown wader with fairly short, grey-green legs and thin bill. The **plain brown back** and **white shoulder patch in the shape of an inverted C** are diagnostic. Common **summer migrant** usually found foraging alone on mudflats or flooded grassland. When walking, the tail is constantly bobbed up and down. In flight, the long **white wingbars** are conspicuous.

Length: 20 cm ss: Ruff (26 cm)

Threebanded Plover

Small plover with plain brown back contrasting with white underparts, and **red eye-ring**. Its name is something of a misnomer, as there are only **two black chest bands**. Occurs singly or in pairs on mudflats where it searches busily for small insects and worms. Frequently confiding. Often associates with migrant waders in summer.

Length: 18 cm ss: Kittlitz's Plover; Whitefronted Plover; Ringed Plover

Blackwinged Stilt

Slender, black and white wader with **extraordinarily long red legs**, and thin pointed bill. Immature birds have grey smudges on the head. Favours mudflats and shallow water, often feeding in the company of larger storks and herons. Frequently bends over to probe the mud for worms and insect larvae. Prone to seasonal movement depending upon water levels.

Length: 38 cm ss: Avocet (42 cm, upturned bill)

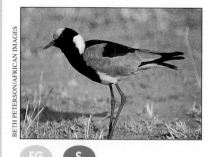

Blacksmith Plover

Black, grey and white plover with dark red eyes. The long legs are grey-black. Occurs in pairs or family groups in open habitats, often near water. Like other plovers, it lays its eggs on bare ground, relying on egg and nestling camouflage for protection. When nests are threatened, the parents rise into the air above the intruders, chanting their metallic 'tink-tink' call.
Length: 30 cm

Longtoed Plover

Black and grey plover with diagnostic **white face**. The long legs are coral-pink. In flight, the wings are completely white apart from black tips. Occurs in pairs or small family groups in aquatic habitats, walking on floating vegetation in the manner of jacanas. Feeds on aquatic insects and small snails. Eggs are laid among grasses or sedges. The call is a series of high-pitched notes.
Length: 30 cm

Wattled Plover

Grey-brown plover with a pair of floppy yellow wattles at the base of the yellow bill. The long **yellow legs** are diagnostic. A small white patch is visible on the crown. Occurs in pairs or small family groups, usually near water. Eggs are laid in short grass or on bare ground. Noisy, but less demonstrative than Crowned or Blacksmith plovers; the call is a high-pitched 'keeep-keeep'.
Length: 35 cm   ss: Whitecrowned Plover

Crowned Plover

Sandy-brown plover with a white under-belly, and **black and white crown**. The long legs are red. Occurs in short grass-land; in pairs when breeding, or flocks during winter. Eggs are laid on the ground. In defence of eggs and young adults circle above intruders, dive-bombing and calling loudly; they may feign injury in order to distract predators from their nest.
Length: 30 cm

African Skimmer

Tern-like bird with black back and white underparts. The unusual **red bill has a protruding lower mandible**. Occurs on rivers and lagoons, breeding on exposed sandbars in the 'pan-handle' between July and October. Lives in small flocks; most active at dusk when they skim the water for small fish. Eggs and chicks are cryptically camouflaged, but vulnerable to trampling and powerboat waves.
Length: 38 cm

WILDERNESS SAFARIS/COLIN BELL

PS   O

Whiskered Tern

Small, pale grey tern with **black cap**, white underwings and red bill and feet. Immatures and non-breeding adults lack the black cap but have a dark streak from eye to nape; the underparts are white and the bill and feet black (non-breeding **Whitewinged Tern** has a dark spot behind the eye). Occurs in pairs or small flocks. Flies in a bouncy manner, diving for small fish. Nests on floating vegetation.
Length: 25 cm   ss: Whitewinged Tern (23 cm)

BRENDAN RYAN

PS   O   FG

Redwinged Pratincole

Tern-like bird with long wings and deeply forked tail. The upperparts are buff-brown and the underparts white. The throat is fawn with a black gorget. In flight, the **white rump** is obvious, the rust-red underwings less so. Flocks of up to 1 000 birds roost on open ground near water and swarm together to hawk small insects, often in the company of **Blackwinged Pratincole**.
Length: 25 cm   ss: Blackwinged Pratincole

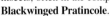

BRENDAN RYAN

FG

Water Dikkop

Nocturnal, plover-like bird occurring on the edges of lagoons and rivers. The large **yellow eyes and long yellow legs** are distinctive. The streaked upperparts, grey wing panel and **white wing bar** separate it from the larger **Spotted Dikkop** (which is found in dry habitats). Occurs in pairs or small groups. The call is a plaintive whistle – 'teee-teee-teeoou' – made after dark. Feeds on insects and small aquatic creatures.
Length: 40 cm   ss: Spotted Dikkop (44 cm)

LEX HES

I   FG

47

Whitebacked Vulture

Large, drab brown vulture with a **long almost bare neck**. Adults become paler with age, ranging from brown to blonde. The **white back** of adults is visible only in flight. The immature is dark brown with pale streaks and lacks the white back. Gregarious scavenger; hundreds may gather to feed at a large carcass. Noisy and quarrelsome. Stick nests are built on the top of a tall tree.
Length: 95 cm

Hooded Vulture

Small, dark brown vulture with a **long thin bill**. The face and throat of the adult is pink, and the leggings white. Immatures have a pale grey face and dark brown leggings. Lives in pairs so invariably out-numbered by other vultures at carcasses. Small flocks may gather at hunting camps. Uniformly dark in flight, it may be confused with the next species. Nest is built in the fork of an evergreen tree.
Length: 70 cm

Lappetfaced Vulture

Huge, dark brown vulture with a pink face and massive, horn-coloured bill. The adult has a **white breast with dark streaks** and **white leggings**. Immature has a pale face and little or no white on the body. Usually in pairs, but dominates other vultures at carcasses. May kill small animals for itself. In flight the **white leggings and 'armpits'** are diagnostic. Nests on top of a low tree.
Length: 1 m   ss: Whiteheaded Vulture

Secretarybird

Large terrestrial raptor with long legs and quill-like plumes protruding from the back of the head. The bare face is orange and the legs are pink. Occurs in pairs in open country where it searches for snakes, lizards and rodents. Runs along ground before taking flight. A pair of elongated tail feathers extend past the tail to provide a distinctive flight outline. Nests on top of a low tree.
Length: 1.4 m

African Fish Eagle

Large, rust-brown eagle with **snow-white head and chest**. The immature is mottled in ash-brown and white. Conspicuous resident of waterways, often located by its evocative 'kyow-kow-kow' call. Pairs often perch within sight of each other in tall trees, swooping down to grasp fish from the water, or to 'pirate' a meal from another bird. Nests below the canopy of a large tree.
Length: 60 to 70 cm

WILDERNESS SAFARIS/COLIN BELL

Bateleur

Stocky, mostly black eagle with **scarlet face and legs**. The back and tail are chestnut. In flight, the female can be told from the male by the much thinner black line on the trailing edge of the **white wings**. The immature is plain brown. Flies as though balancing on a tightrope, with feet protruding beyond the **extremely short tail**. Feeds on small animals and carrion. Nests on a low branch of a large tree.
Length: 60 cm ss: Longcrested Eagle

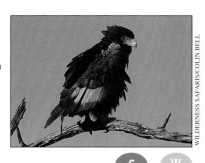

WILDERNESS SAFARIS/COLIN BELL

Martial Eagle

Huge eagle with **white breast finely spotted in brown**, and dark brown back and head peaked with a small crest. The eyes are yellow. In flight, the **dark underwings** are diagnostic. Immature is pure white below and pale grey on the back. Preys on animals up to the size of Steenbok. Nests below the canopy of a tall tree.
Length: 80 cm ss: Blackbreasted Snake Eagle (65 cm, white underwings, unspotted breast)

PETER HANCOCK

Gymnogene

Large, pale grey raptor with broad wings and small head. The **bare face** is yellow, but becomes pink when excited. The underparts are finely barred. In flight, the **black tail, with a single, broad, white band**, is diagnostic. The immature is brown and buff, and can be confused with other raptors. The long yellow legs are double-jointed and used to extract prey from holes. Nests in a tall tree.
Length: 60 cm ss: Dark Chanting Goshawk (52 cm)

LEX HES

49

Tawny Eagle

Large eagle with variable plumage. Some birds are rich rufous in colour, others pale blonde, but most are tawny-brown. Females are often darker than males. The feet and cere are yellow and the leggings shaggy. Preys and scavenges on a variety of small animals and often pirates kills of other birds. Nests on top of a tall tree.
Length: 70 cm ss: Steppe Eagle (75 cm, summer migrant); Lesser Spotted Eagle (65 cm, summer migrant); Brown Snake Eagle (74 cm)

Wahlberg's Eagle

Small eagle with plumage varying from dark brown to blonde, but usually medium brown. When perched, the diagnostic **small crest** is visible at the back of the head. In flight, the comparatively long **tail is usually held closed** (rather than fanned). Preys on small animals from gamebirds to flying termites, but not known to scavenge. Summer migrant, nesting below the canopy of a tree.
Length: 58 cm ss: Longcrested Eagle (all black)

Yellowbilled Kite

Dark brown raptor with long dexterous wings. The **broad triangular tail**, often held in a V-shape, is diagnostic. The legs, cere and bill of the adult are yellow. The immature has a black bill, as does the similar **Black Kite** – which can be told apart by its grey head. Often scavenges, so is frequently found around villages. Nests under the canopy of a leafy tree. **Summer migrant**.
Length: 56 cm ss: Steppe Buzzard (45-50 cm)

African Marsh Harrier

Brown raptor with streaky plumage and long bare legs. The **forewings are rimmed in white**. The immature has an off-white chest bar. The eyes are bright yellow. Always associated with aquatic habitats, it typically flies low and with deep wing beats above wetlands. Feeds on a variety of water-associated birds, rodents, snakes and frogs. Nests on the ground among reeds or papyrus.
Length: 47 cm ss: Montague's Harrier

Blackshouldered Kite ✓

Small, pale grey raptor with snow-white head and underparts and diagnostic **black shoulder patches**. The feet and cere are yellow and the eyes bright red. The immature is blotched in ash-brown and white. Often perches on the highest available point and typically wags its tail. Regularly hovers above grassland. Rodents are the main prey. The nest is built in a shrub or tree.

Length: 33 cm

FG S

Gabar Goshawk

Small, pale grey raptor with **red legs and cere** and dark eyes. The throat and upper chest are grey, with **grey barring only on the belly**. Young birds are brown and blotched but – like the adults – have a distinctive **white rump**. An all-black, melanistic form occurs. Feeds mostly on small birds. The nest is built in a thorny bush. Perches within canopy.

Length: 32 cm ss: Little Banded Goshawk (30 cm); Lizard Buzzard (36 cm); Little Sparrowhawk (24 cm)

LEX HES

S W

Rednecked Falcon

Small grey raptor with **chestnut crown and neck**, and dark 'tear-streaks' below eyes. The throat is white, merging to cream with fine black barring on the belly. In flight, the pointed wings and black band toward the end of the white-tipped tail are distinctive. Preys on small birds up to the size of a dove. Nests in the crown of a Fan Palm or the old stick nest of a crow. Usually perches below canopy.

Length: 35 cm ss: Lanner Falcon (45 cm)

S

Dickinson's Kestrel

Small, dark grey raptor with **pale grey head** and black eyes. In flight, the long pointed wings are distinctive. The tail and underwings are strongly barred. Favours open country, including flood-plains. Prey ranges from insects to small birds and rodents, and is usually cap-tured on the ground. Normally breeds in the crown of a Fan Palm or a cavity in a Baobab.

Length: 30 cm ss: Western Redfooted Kestrel

BRENDAN RYAN

FG S

51

Redbilled Francolin

Ash-brown francolin with finely barred underparts and **yellow eye-rings**. The bill and legs are coral-red. The immature has a black bill. Favours dry, open areas. May be confiding around camps where it picks up crumbs. The harsh call is made at dusk and dawn. Often perches on termite mounds. Feeds primarily on insects and seeds. The eggs are laid on the ground in long grass.
Length: 35 cm

Swainson's Francolin

Dark brown francolin with streaked plumage and **bare red skin around the eyes**. The upper bill and legs are black. The harsh, crowing call is often made from a termite mound or branch of a tree. Prefers denser vegetation than the Redbilled Francolin, but the two may occur side by side. Nervous and quick to retreat into cover. Feeds mostly on berries, seeds and insects.
Length: 38 cm

Crested Francolin

Fawn, rust and cream francolin with a broad **white eye-stripe** and dark line through the eye. The crown is dark, the bill grey and the legs are pink-orange. Occurs in pairs or family parties, often coming out into the open on sand tracks. Calls excitedly at dawn, less often at dusk. Termites and other insects are the chief food. Eggs are laid on the ground amongst dense vegetation.
Length: 33 cm   ss: Coqui Francolin (24 cm)

Helmeted Guineafowl

Distinctive, charcoal-grey bird profusely spotted in white. The bare facial skin is predominantly blue, with a variable amount of red around the eyes. A horny casque – in the shape of a helmet – sits on the crown. Lives in flocks in dry woodland, and is particularly abundant along the Chobe River. Feeds on termites, beetles and seeds. Eggs are laid on the ground amongst dense vegetation.
Length: 56 cm

Kori Bustard

Huge, grey-brown bustard with white underparts and neck finely barred in grey. Weighing up to 19 kg, it is said to be the heaviest flying bird. A small black crest protrudes from the back of the head. Favours open country where it strides slowly in search of insects, lizards and seeds. The dramatic courtship display includes the puffing-out of the neck feathers. Eggs are laid near a grass tuft.
Length: 1.3 m

Redcrested Korhaan

Small slender bustard with speckled brown back marked with diagnostic **white V-patterns**, and black underbelly. Males have grey necks. Despite its name, the red crest is only visible in displaying males, which also engage in dramatic aerial courtship displays. The call is a drawn-out piping whistle. Occurs in pairs. Shy, but relies on camouflage and often stands motionless when detected.
Length: 50 cm ss: Blackbellied Korhaan (64 cm)

LEX HES

Ground Hornbill

Huge black hornbill with massive bill. Bare skin around the eyes and throat of the adult is red; the female has a blue patch on the throat. The immature has pale yellow facial skin. When airborne, the white flight feathers are conspicuous. Lives in family groups of up to seven which walk along in search of prey such as tortoises and snakes. The call is a deep 'oooom'. Nests in a large tree hole.
Length: 90 cm

MARK TENNANT/AFRICAN IMAGES

Fierynecked Nightjar

Nocturnal bird with cryptic, brown and fawn plumage. Rarely seen, and known mostly by its beautiful call – often described as 'good Lord, deliver us'. Most vociferous during the dry season, and particularly on moonlit nights. **Roosts and perches on branches**, seldom alighting on the ground. Moths and other insects are captured on the wing.
Length: 24 cm ss: Rufoucheeked Nightjar; Natal (Swamp) Nightjar; Mozambique Nightjar

LEX HES

Doublebanded Sandgrouse

Pigeon-like bird with **pointed wings**. The male is speckled on the back with a sandy breast rimmed with two bars in black and white. The eye is surrounded by bare yellow skin, and the forehead is black and white. Females are cryptically coloured. Usually in pairs, but flocks gather to drink at dusk. Eggs are laid on the ground.

Length: 25 cm ss: Burchell's Sandgrouse; Yellowthroated Sandgrouse

Mourning Dove

Large, grey-headed dove with bold black collar. The breast is pinkish, and the **pale yellow eyes** are surrounded by bare red skin. The similar **Redeyed Dove** is larger, with a pale pink head and red eyes. Occurs in large trees close to water and is often common around camps. The soft 'kook-kurrrr' call gives this bird its name. The small twig nest is often built in a thorn tree. Feeds on seeds.

Length: 30 cm ss: Redeyed Dove (35 cm)

Cape Turtle Dove

Medium-sized, pale grey dove with black neck collar finely edged in white. The **black eyes and pale grey breast** tell it apart from the previous species. The evocative 'kuk-cooo-kuk' call is one of Africa's typical sounds. Usually found in pairs, but may gather in large flocks at water in the dry season. Small twig nest is built within a shrub or tree. Seeds are the main food.

Length: 28 cm

Laughing Dove

Small, brick-red and grey dove with pink head and breast speckled in black. Common and widespread in the more open habitats and, like other doves, dependent on drinking water. Most often found in pairs but may form flocks at waterholes. The call is a soft cooing, often uttered at midday. May be tame in camps, gardens and towns. Feeds mostly on seeds. The nest is a small twig structure.

Length: 26 cm

Namaqua Dove

Small dove with distinctive long tail. The male has a **black mask and throat**, and **yellow bill** with a red base; female has a uniform grey head and throat. Both sexes have small indigo-blue wing-spots. In flight, the **chestnut wings** are distinctive. Occurs in pairs or small flocks in sparsely vegetated areas. Nomadic, with numbers fluctuating in relation to rainfall. The call is a double-note hoot.
Length: 28 cm

Greenspotted Dove

Small, cinnamon-brown dove with pale forehead. Four or five **emerald-green spots** are displayed on the closed wing. In flight, the **chestnut wings** are distinctive. The descending call – 'doo-doo-du-du-dududu' – is one of Africa's most evocative sounds. Shyer than other doves, but frequently seen on quiet sand roads. The twig nest is often built in an exposed site. Seeds are the main food.
Length: 22 cm

African Green Pigeon

Parrot-like dove with olive-green back, grey-green head and lemon-yellow underparts. The eye is pale mauve, the base of the bill and feet red, and the leggings are bright yellow. Feeds mostly on figs but takes most soft fruits. Small flocks are often seen flying in and out of large trees. Frail twig nests are built in tall trees. The call is a series of clicking notes followed by liquid whistles.
Length: 30 cm

Meyer's Parrot

Small brown parrot with **turquoise-green underparts and rump**, and a variable amount of bright yellow on the shoulders, underwing and forehead. Occurs in small flocks which often draw attention to themselves by their shrill, piercing calls. Flies speedily with rapid wingbeats. Seedpods are the favoured food, but soft fruit is also eaten. The eggs are laid in a tree hole or cavity.
Length: 22 cm

55

ILLUSTRATIVE OPTIONS

PS

Copperytailed Coucal

Large, chestnut-winged bird with cream underparts and broad, floppy black tail. The **upper tail feathers are finely barred**, and the eyes are bright red. Occurs in **permanent swamp** where its bubbling call is a characteristic sound. Often seen in the early morning, perched out in the open. Rarely visits dryer bush. Diet includes aquatic insects, frogs and nestling birds. Occurs singly or in pairs.
Length: 48 cm

ILLUSTRATIVE OPTIONS

 W   S

Senegal Coucal

Medium-sized, chestnut-winged bird with cream underparts and broad, floppy black tail. The **upper tail feathers are unbarred**, and the eyes are bright red. Avoids permanent swamps, preferring to forage in dryer bush. The bubbling call is indistinguishable from that of the previous species. Suns itself in exposed positions; flies clumsily between bush clumps. A wide variety of prey is taken.
Length: 40 cm ss: Whitebrowed Coucal; Black Coucal

RF   FG   W

Diederik Cuckoo

Small, coppery-green cuckoo with snow-white underparts. The male is metallic green above, with red eyes surrounded by red skin. The female is bronze above, spotted in buff. The immature has an orange bill. A **summer migrant** from central Africa. Its name is derived from the repetitive call – 'di-di-deederik'. Eggs are laid in the nests of sparrows, weavers and bishops.
Length: 18 cm ss: Klaas's Cuckoo

 S   W

Grey Lourie

Large, ash-grey bird with distinctive **crest of lacy feathers and long tail**. Occurs in pairs during the breeding season, but flocks may gather around waterholes in the dry winter months. Most common in dry savanna, but never far from water. The call is a nasal 'gweeeh' (go away) – often uttered in alarm. Feeds mostly on berries and leaf buds. The nest is a bowl of twigs set in a thorn tree.
Length: 48 cm

Pel's Fishing Owl

Huge ginger owl with dark streaks and black eyes. The immature is paler with a cream-coloured head. Feeds almost exclusively on fish, so is always found near water – quiet inlets with overhanging branches are preferred. Nocturnal, but may perch in the open in the early morning. Roosts by day within a densely foliaged tree. Shy and wary. Call is a deep grunt or an eerie wail.

Length: 63 cm

Giant Eagle Owl

Huge, grey-brown owl with pale face rimmed in black, and diagnostic **pink eyelids** above black eyes. The ear-tufts create a cat-like silhouette. Young birds are paler with fine barring. Occurs in pairs, often along watercourses. Eggs are normally laid in an abandoned eagle nest. Smaller mammals and birds up to the size of Helmeted Guineafowl are the prey. Call is a deep 'ooomph' grunt.

Length: 65 cm   ss: Spotted Eagle Owl (45 cm)

Scops Owl

Tiny, cryptically plumaged owl with ear tufts and yellow eyes. The back is blotched and the breast streaked. Roosts by day against the trunk of a tree – Knobthorn and Mopane are favoured – where it is superbly camouflaged. The repetitive 'pruuup' call is one of Africa's most evocative night sounds. Feeds primarily on insects, caught in flight or on the ground. Eggs are laid in a small tree hole.

Length: 20 cm   ss: Whitefaced Owl (28 cm)

Barred Owl

Small chubby owl with boldly **barred, rufous back** and head, and yellow eyes. The white underbelly is blotched in brown. Prefers dense vegetation, often occurring near water. Feeds on insects, spiders and small rodents. Eggs are laid in a tree hole. Call is a dove-like 'kurrr', made only at night. The **Pearlspotted Owl** has **white spots on the head** and back, and streaks on the white underbelly; it prefers open areas and calls by day.

Length: 21 cm   ss: Pearlspotted Owl (18 cm)

Redfaced Mousebird

Small, pale grey, mouse-like bird with a long tail. The underparts are buffy. The **bright red facial skin** is diagnostic. Occurs in small flocks which usually fly together, and speedily, from one place to the next. Birds huddle together at their roost. Soft fruit and berries are the main food. A small stick nest is built within a tangled bush or creeper. Call is a clear whistle.

Length: 34 cm

Giant Kingfisher

Massive, charcoal-grey kingfisher with white-spotted back. Sexes differ in that the **male has only the breast rufous**, while the **female is rufous on the underbelly and underwings**. Feeds mostly on crabs, but also takes fish and frogs. Fishes alone or in pairs. The loud 'khak-khak-khak' call is often made in flight. The nest is a tunnel excavated in a steep river bank or termite mound.

Length: 46 cm

Pied Kingfisher

Medium-sized, black and white kingfisher. The white underparts are divided by a **double chest bar in the male**, and a **single broken bar in the female**. Hunts for fish by hovering above water and plunging in after prey. Occurs in pairs or family groups, and nests in a sandbank burrow. Most frequently seen kingfisher in the region and often shows little fear of people. Call is a series of twitters.

Length: 28 cm

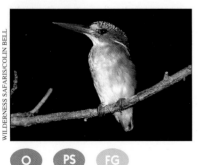

Malachite Kingfisher

Tiny, jewel-like kingfisher with bright blue back, chestnut underparts and **scarlet bill**. The crest is the colour of malachite stone, banded in black. Sexes are alike. The immature is duller and has a black bill. Perches low among reeds and sedges alongside water where small fish, frogs, tadpoles and aquatic insects are caught. Call is a high-pitched whistle. Nests in a burrow in a sandbank.

Length: 14 cm ss: Halfcollared Kingfisher (20 cm)

Woodland Kingfisher

Medium-sized, turquoise-blue kingfisher with **black shoulders** and **red and black bill**. Immature is duller with shorter, reddish-brown bill. Like the next species, this kingfisher does not fish, but feeds on large insects and lizards. Favours open areas with tall trees, breeding in woodpecker or barbet holes. A **summer migrant** from central Africa. Call is a piercing, repetitive trill – 'tri-tri-trirrrrrrr'.

Length: 23 cm ss: Greyhooded Kingfisher

Striped Kingfisher

Small, dark-backed kingfisher with blue wings and tail. A **black stripe runs through the eye**, the pale chest is streaked and the bill dull red. Favours open woodland, where it hunts for insects and small lizards. The eggs are laid in an abandoned woodpecker hole in summer. Call is a repetitive 'chee-cherrrr', most often made at dusk and frequently accompanied by open wing displays.

Length: 18 cm ss: Brownhooded Kingfisher

Lilacbreasted Roller

Brilliantly coloured roller with **electric blue wings and tail** – most distinctive in flight. The breast and cheeks are lilac. Streamers protrude beyond the tail. Occurs in pairs in open areas, perching conspicuously on dead trees and termite mounds. Summer courtship display involves aerial rolls and tumbles. Eggs are laid in a tree hole nest. Prey includes large insects and lizards.

Length: 36 cm ss: European Roller (summer visitor)

WILDERNESS SAFARIS/COLIN BELL

Broadbilled Roller

Small cinnamon roller with indigo wings and bright blue tail. The **broad yellow bill** is diagnostic. **Summer migrant**, breeding in holes in dead trees, often near water. Noisy and aggressive around the nest. Usually seen in pairs, but flocks assemble on passage. Feeds on a variety of flying insects, often at dusk when it may be mistaken for a nightjar or fruit bat. The call is a harsh croak.

Length: 27 cm ss: Purple Roller (38 cm, black bill)

IAN SUTHERLAND/AFRICAN IMAGES

Little Bee-eater

Small, green-backed bee-eater with fawn underparts and yellow throat with black collar. A thin blue eyebrow is present. The **square tail** is green and buff with a black tip. Occurs in pairs or family groups in open woodland and on floodplains. Hawks butterflies and other flying insects from low perch. Nests away from water in earth bank or termite mound. Call is a soft tinkling note.
Length: 18 cm

S FG PS

Swallowtailed Bee-eater

Small green bee-eater with yellow throat terminating in pale blue collar. The **deeply forked tail** and rump are turquoise-blue. Occurs in pairs or family groups, typically on the fringe of broad-leaved woodland. Bees and other flying insects are the chief prey. The nest is a burrow in a low bank, sometimes on level ground. Call is a series of soft twittering notes.
Length: 22 cm

W

Bluecheeked Bee-eater

Large, **bright green** bee-eater with blue forehead, eyebrow and cheeks. The throat is yellow. A pair of streamers protrudes beyond the tail of the adult. The immature is duller. Non-breeding **summer migrant** from the Middle East, most common on floodplains and papyrus beds along channels. Occurs in small flocks. Dragonflies are the main prey. The call is a liquid 'prrrup'.
Length: 31 cm

FG PS

European Bee-eater

Large, **golden-backed** bee-eater with turquoise wings, tail and underparts. The yellow throat is fringed with a black collar. A pair of streamers protrudes beyond the tail of the adult. The immature is duller. Non-breeding **summer migrant** from the Mediterranean. Occurs in flocks of up to 100 in open habitats. Feeds mostly on bees but, like other bee-eaters, swarms around grass fires to snap up fleeing grasshoppers. The call is a liquid 'prrrup'.
Length: 28 cm

S W FG

Carmine Bee-eater

Large, bright pink bee-eater with turquoise cap, and blue rump and vent. Like all bee-eaters, a black mask runs through the eye. Young birds are dull pink and lack the long tail streamers of adults. Soars with pointed wings, snapping up bees and other insects. Gregarious **summer migrant**, breeding in colonies of up to 100 pairs in sandbank burrows. Call is a rolling 'trrerrk-trrerrk'.
Length: 36 cm

Whitefronted Bee-eater

Medium-sized, green-backed bee-eater. The **throat is red**, forehead white and **vent bright blue**. A white band runs below the black mask. The **square tail lacks streamers**. Immatures are duller. Prefers well-wooded areas, usually near water. Breeds in colonies of up to 20 pairs in sandbank burrows, sometimes alongside the previous species. Flying insects are the prey. Call is a nasal 'squerr'.
Length: 24 cm

Hoopoe

Distinctive, brick-red bird with black and white wings and a fan-shaped crest. The long curved bill is used for probing the ground for worms and insects. In flight it resembles a giant butterfly. Usually seen singly or in pairs, less often in family groups; favours dryer open areas. Nests in a cavity in a tree, often quite low to the ground. The call is a repetitive 'hoop-hoop-hoop'.
Length: 28 cm

Redbilled Woodhoopoe

Long-tailed, ink-blue bird with a metallic green sheen. The long **curved bill and short legs are coral-red**. An active and noisy bird which lives in family groups of five or more. The cackling call is made in unison and often culminates with all the birds rocking back and forth on branches. Insect larvae are extracted from under the bark of trees. Young are reared in a tree hole.
Length: 36 cm ss: Greater Scimitarbill (26 cm)

BRENDAN RYAN

61

Yellowbilled Hornbill

Medium-sized, black and white hornbill with distinctive **yellow bill**. The bare skin around the pale yellow eyes is red, as is the throat patch. Favours open, dry habitats, spending much time on the ground in search of beetles. Nests in a tree cavity, with the female enclosing herself with the eggs. The hollow call – 'toka-toka-toka' – is made with the head lowered and wings raised.
Length: 55 cm

Redbilled Hornbill

Small, black and white hornbill with distinctive **red bill**. There is no bare skin on the face. Favours broad-leaved woodland, especially mature Mopane, but may occur alongside the Yellowbilled Hornbill. Spends much time on the ground in search of beetles. Nests in a tree hole, with the female enclosing herself with the eggs. The call is a series of clucking notes.
Length: 46 cm

Bradfield's Hornbill

Medium-sized, grey-brown hornbill with an **orange** bill. The pale yellow eye is set within a dark facial mask. The underbelly and tips of the tail feathers are white. Occurs in pairs or small groups in broad-leaved woodland, particularly Zambezi Teak. Insect prey is taken on the ground. Nests in a tree hole, with the female enclosing herself with the eggs. The call is a repeated whistle.
Length: 56 cm

Grey Hornbill

Small, grey and white hornbill with a bold **white eye-stripe**. The bill of the male is black with a yellow panel and a small casque, while that of the female is horn-coloured with a maroon tip. Occurs in pairs when breeding but may form small flocks during the dry season. Insects and berries make up the bulk of the diet. The dipping flight and plaintive whistled call are distinctive.
Length: 46 cm

Blackcollared Barbet

Stocky barbet with **crimson-red face** bordered by a **black collar**. The back is olive-green and the underparts buffy-yellow. The stout **black bill** is used to excavate nest holes in the branches of trees. Noisy and conspicuous, it occurs in pairs or family groups. The call is a repetitive 'duduloo-duduloo' in duet or chorus. Insects, berries and fruit – especially figs – are the favoured food.
Length: 20 cm

Crested Barbet

Multi-coloured barbet with **yellow and red underparts and face**, and black back blotched in white. The stout **pale bill** is used to excavate nest holes in the branches of trees. The ragged crest is raised when the alarm clock-trill call is made. Occurs in pairs in dryer, more open habitats. Fruit and berries are the favoured food, but ground-dwelling insects are also eaten.
Length: 23 cm

Bearded Woodpecker

Large, olive-backed woodpecker with **pale grey underparts barred in white**. The male has a scarlet crown and finely spotted forehead; the female has no red on the head. The white face has broad black streaks behind the eye and below the bill. Usually seen in pairs in the branches of taller trees. The call is a rapid 'wik-wik-wik' or a resonant drumming. Eggs are laid in a self-made tree hole.
Length: 26 cm ss: Bennett's Woodpecker (24 cm)

Cardinal Woodpecker

Small, olive-backed woodpecker with **white underparts streaked in brown**. The male has a scarlet crown while that of the female is black. Both sexes have a diagnostic **plain brown forehead**, and a single dark streak running from the base of the bill. Occurs in pairs, often in mixed bird parties. Nests in a self-made tree hole. Call is series of 'kree-kree' notes. Insect larvae are the main food.
Length: 15 cm ss: Goldentailed Woodpecker (23 cm)

Lesser Striped Swallow

Blue-black swallow with **orange head and face**, and pale breast lined with bold black streaks. Occurs in pairs or small flocks, usually near water. Feeds on the wing, taking small insects such as gnats and flies. Call is a series of nasal mewing notes. Mud pellet nest is built under bridges, eaves or the branches of trees. May become tame and confiding. **Summer migrant** from central Africa.

Length: 16 cm ss: Greater Striped Swallow (20 cm)

LEX HES

Wiretailed Swallow

Blue-black swallow with **orange cap** and snow-white underparts. The wire-like tail streamers are so thin as to be almost invisible. Occurs in pairs or small groups, invariably near water. Feeds on the wing, taking small insects such as gnats and flies. Call is an excited 'chisik-chisik'. Mud pellet nest is built under bridges, verandas or the branches of trees overhanging water.

Length: 13 cm ss: Whitethroated Swallow

European Swallow

Blue-black swallow with chestnut forehead and throat, **broad black collar** and cream underparts. Immature is dusky. Gregarious, non-breeding **summer migrant** from Europe. Flocks of up to 200 hawk flying insects in open habitats. Night-time roosts in reedbeds may host thousands of birds. Prior to heading north in March-April, large numbers assemble on trees and overhead wires.

Length: 18 cm

JOHN CARLYON

Greyrumped Swallow

Blue-black swallow with paler head, **pale grey rump** and cream underparts. More frequently seen during the winter months. Occurs in flocks of up to 30. Hawks small insects above short grassland, especially in recently burnt areas, and often adjacent to water. Breeding is unusual in that it occurs during winter; the eggs are laid in a burrow on level ground.

Length: 14 cm ss: House Martin

Brownthroated Martin

Dull brown swallow which occurs in two colour forms: one with a white underbelly and vent, the other all brown. The **square tail** lacks streamers. Occurs in small flocks of up to 20, almost always near water. Hawks small flying insects above the surface. Eggs are laid in holes in vertical riverbanks. The call is a series of weak twittering notes. Populations are subject to seasonal movements.

Length: 13 cm ss: Sand Martin; Banded Martin

Palm Swift

Ash-brown swift differing from the previous species (and all swallows) in its more rapid flight, and **long, sickle-shaped wings**. The long tail is deeply forked. Occurs in small flocks wherever Fan Palms grow, and around ornamental palm trees in towns. The nest is affixed to palm fronds, and the eggs are secured with a sticky secretion.

Length: 17 cm ss: European Swift (black)

Pied Crow

Large, glossy black bird with **white breast and collar**. In this region it is largely restricted to settlements such as Maun, Kasane and Katima Mulilo. Can be expected to increase in numbers as villages expand. Scavenges around dumps and frequently feeds on road kills. Bulky stick nest is often built in man-made structures such as towers and electricity pylons.

Length: 50 cm ss: Black Crow

Blackheaded Oriole

Bright, sulphur-yellow bird with greenish back and black head. The **bill and eyes are coral-red**. Immature has a speckled head. Favours well-wooded habitats where it occurs singly or in pairs. Often joins mixed bird parties during winter. Insects and caterpillars are caught within the foliage of large trees. Call is a liquid 'pleeoo' whistle, or a harsh nasal alarm. Cup nest is adorned with lichen.

Length: 24 cm ss: African Golden Oriole (black eye mask); European Golden Oriole (black wings)

W RF

Greater Honeyguide

Drab, brown and buff bird with distinctive **white outer tail feathers** most obvious in **dipping flight**. Male has a pale pink bill, black throat and white ear patch. Immature has a dark back and pale yellow underparts. May guide people to bee-hives, and feeds on bee larvae and wax. Male calls 'whit-purr' monotonously from a territorial tree-top perch. Calls mostly during summer.
Length: 20 cm

S

Rufousnaped Lark

Mottled, tawny-fawn bird with **pale eye-stripe and pointed crest**. The wings are chestnut-red; obvious in flight or in perched birds. Forages and nests on the ground but perches conspicuously on a low bush or termite mound. Call is a drawn-out 'tseeu-tseeuoo' whistle. The crest of loose feathers may be raised in alarm or when calling. Usually seen singly.
Length: 18 cm ss: Flappet Lark; Fawncoloured Lark

Grassland (Richard's) Pipit

Small, ground-dwelling bird similar in colour to the previous species, but with a lighter build. The **white outer tail feathers** are conspicuous in flight. Occurs in open short grassland including airstrips. Calls 'cri-chri-chri' during a dipping display flight. The similar Plainbacked Pipit has buff outer tail feathers and an unstreaked back; it prefers damp floodplains.
Length: 16 cm ss: Plainbacked Pipit

S FG

Yellowbellied Bulbul

Secretive bulbul with pale olive head and back, and **lemon-yellow underparts and underwings**. The eyes are fringed with thin white eyebrows. Occurs in pairs or small family groups along permanent watercourses. A resident of many camps and lodges, it may become tame and confiding. The call is a nasal 'nye-nye-nye', often in chorus by the family group.
Length: 23 cm ss: Terrestrial Bulbul

RF

Blackeyed Bulbul

Lively bulbul with brown back, pale underparts and distinctive **yellow vent**. The black head has a small crest which gives a peaked appearance. Occurs in pairs or family groups in well-wooded areas. Confiding and often found in the vicinity of lodges and camps. The call is a series of liquid whistles, but the 'cheet-cheet-cheet' alarm call is better known. Small insects and berries are eaten.
Length: 22 cm ss: Redeyed Bulbul

LEX HES

Pied Babbler

Striking, **snow-white** babbler with **black wings and tail**. The bill is black and the eyes golden-brown. Immature is buffy-fawn. Occurs in family parties, usually in dry scrubby vegetation with acacia trees. Spends much time on the ground searching for beetles and other insect prey. Groups engage in raucous, high-pitched babbling sessions. Nest is built within tangled vegetation.
Length: 26 cm

Arrowmarked Babbler

Drab brown bird with bright orange eyes and **bold white streaks – in the shape of arrows – on the crown, throat and chest**. Immature lacks white streaks and is paler overall. Favours tangled vegetation and is less often seen than heard. Gregarious and noisy; the call is a raucous cackle – not unlike that of the Redbilled Woodhoopoe – uttered in unison by groups of up to 12 birds.
Length: 24 cm

Hartlaub's Babbler

Drab brown bird with red eyes, **white rump and vent** and **pale head**. Feathers of the mantle, head and underparts are rimmed in white, giving a **scaly appearance**. Favours tangled growth alongside water including stands of papyrus and reedbeds. Gregarious and noisy; the call is a raucous cackle made by groups of up to 12 birds. Also known as the **Whiterumped Babbler**.
Length: 26 cm

67

Heuglin's Robin

Bright orange robin with slate-grey back. The black head is divided by a bold white eye-stripe. Immature is heavily speckled. Occurs in pairs. May become confiding around camps and lodges, but is otherwise secretive. Extremely vociferous – the strident dawn and dusk call is a series of clear whistled notes; a churring alarm may also be uttered. Feeds on insects caught among leaf litter.
Length: 20 cm

JOHN CARLYON

Whitebrowed Scrub Robin

Small brown robin with white **underparts heavily streaked** in dark brown. The bold white eye-stripes and white wing bars are distinctive. The long tail is chestnut at the base, merging to black and tipped in white; it is raised up and down to reveal the white vent. Avoids dense woodland, preferring open scrub with acacia. Call is a flutey whistle, made mostly at dawn and dusk.
Length: 15 cm ss: Kalahari Robin

Kurrichane Thrush

Grey-brown thrush with **orange bill** and orange-buff underparts. The faintly speckled white throat has a pair of black, moustache-like streaks. Immature is paler, mottled and streaked in buff. Spends most of the time on the ground, searching through leaves for insects and worms. Often feeds on lawns around camps and lodges. Call is a clear 'tseeeou' whistle.
Length: 22 cm

LEX HES

Groundscraper Thrush

Grey-backed thrush with **white underparts boldly streaked in black**. The face is white with distinctive black stripes behind the eyes. In flight, the **buffy wing panels** are distinctive. Immature has scaly appearance to the back, and less obvious streaking. Occurs in pairs in open areas where it feeds on insects. Stands in an **upright posture**. The call is a sequence of whistled notes.
Length: 22 cm ss: Dusky Lark

Arnot's Chat

Small black bird with **white cap and white shoulders**. The female lacks the white cap, but has a white throat and upper breast. Immature has a black head. Occurs in pairs or small family groups in mature Mopane woodland, and to a lesser extent in Zambezi Teak woodland. Forages for insects on the branches and trunks of trees, and also on the ground. The call is a weak squeaky whistle.
Length: 18 cm

Southern Black Tit

Small black bird with **white shoulder patches** and **white edges to the wing feathers**. The female is dusky-grey rather than black. Differs from the previous species with its longer tail, black head and restless behaviour. Pairs or small groups clamber through tangled vegetation and hang from bark in search of insects. Call is a harsh 'cherr-cherr-cherr'. Often found in mixed bird parties.
Length: 16 cm

Forktailed Drongo

Glossy black bird with **deeply forked tail**. Females are greyish below. The **red eyes** are diagnostic. The **hooked bill** has long bristles at its base. In flight, the **wings are noticeably paler than the body**. Occurs singly or in pairs in most habitats. Hawks insects from an exposed perch, often alongside large mammals. Call is a jumble of grating metallic notes. It frequently mobs eagles and hawks.
Length: 25 cm

Black Flycatcher

Glossy black bird with **square or slightly notched tail**. The eyes are dark brown. When perched, the **brown edges to the wing feathers** can be seen. The bill is not strongly hooked. Occurs singly or in pairs in well-wooded habitats. Insects are hawked from an exposed perch but usually captured on the ground. Call is a soft twitter. Unobtrusive, but confiding and often seen around camps and lodges.
Length: 19 cm ss: Black Cuckooshrike

Spotted Flycatcher

Small, pale brown bird with off-white underparts. The name is misleading, as the **breast and forehead are finely streaked**, not spotted. Typically perches low down on the outermost branches of a tree or shrub, launching out to catch flying insects. **Flicks wings on alighting**. Solitary, quiet and inconspicuous. Non-breeding summer migrant from Europe.
Length: 14 cm ss: Mousecoloured Flycatcher; Bluegrey Flycatcher

Marico Flycatcher

Small, brown-backed bird with **snow-white throat and underparts**. Immature is spotted on the back and has brown streaks on the breast. Perches conspicuously at the top or edge of bushes or small trees. Insect prey is often caught on the ground, but taken back to the perch to be eaten. Favours dry scrub with thorn trees, usually in pairs or groups of three. Call is a soft 'schruup'.
Length: 18 cm ss: Mousecoloured Flycatcher

Paradise Flycatcher

Small, **chestnut-backed** bird with indigo-blue head and smoky-grey underparts merging to white vent. The bill and eye wattles are turquoise-blue. Breeding male differs from female in extravagant **ribbon-like tail**. Occurs in pairs. Tiny, egg-cup nest is often conspicuous at the tip of a branch. Call is a gentle 'wee-we-diddly' or a 'jweet' alarm. **Summer migrant**, but some may overwinter.
Length: 15 cm (plus 18 cm tail in breeding male)

Stone Chat

Small squat bird. Male is boldly patterned with chocolate back, black head, **white neck collar** and chestnut breast. Female is mottled on the back with grey head, and fawn breast and underparts. Both have distinctive **white rump and wing bars** in flight. Perches conspicuously in low vegetation or on edges of reedbeds, coming to ground for insects. Solitary or in pairs. Call is a grating 'tsik-tsik'.
Length: 14 cm

Chinspot Batis

Tiny black and white bird with grey crown and mantle. **Bright yellow eyes are set in a black mask**. The male has a broad black bar on the breast, the female a chestnut breast bar and spot on the throat. Immature is mottled. Usually seen in pairs, moving methodically through branches in search of insects. Call is a clear 'di-di-deee' (three blind mice), or a harsh alarm.

Length: 13 cm ss: Brubru (15 cm)

Longbilled Crombec

Tiny, grey-brown bird with buffy underparts and **short, almost non-existent tail**. The thin bill is downcurved. Occurs in pairs, often in the company of other species in mixed bird parties. Moves restlessly among foliage, often hanging upside-down to explore bark for insects. Call is a persistent 'chree-rit'.

Length: 12 cm ss: Burntnecked Eremomela (10 cm, faint chestnut throat bar, sizeable tail); Grey Penduline Tit (8 cm)

Greybacked Bleating Warbler

Tiny, grey-backed bird with pale underparts and **olive-green wings** obvious in flight or at rest. Lively and restless, the tail is constantly flicked and raised to reveal the white vent. Occurs singly or in pairs in dense undergrowth, often near the ground; secretive and seldom seen. Extremely vociferous, the call is a bleating 'bleeep-bleeep' or 'chirrup-chirrup' – surprisingly strident for so small a bird.

Length: 12 cm ss: Stierling's Barred Warbler

Cape Wagtail

Small, long-tailed bird with ash-grey head and back, and thin white eye-stripe. Individuals in this region lack the breast bar characteristic of birds to the south. Occurs singly or in pairs near water, or on moist grassland or lawns. Moves restlessly in search of small insects; the tail is bobbed up and down. **African Pied Wagtail** is black and white and largely confined to the Kwando-Chobe River.

Length: 18 cm ss: African Pied Wagtail (20 cm)

LEX HES

Rattling Cisticola

Dryland cisticola with rufous and black upperparts and pale underparts. Noisy and conspicuous, it perches prominently on a low bush or in rank grass. The call is a distinctive 'tchi-tchi-tchi-trrrrrrr'. Prefers open woodland. The similar **Tinkling Cisticola** has a chestnut-orange tail and cap, prefers semi-arid acacia scrub, and its call is a series of bell-like notes.

Length: 15 cm ss: Tinkling Cisticola (14 cm)

PS

Chirping Cisticola

Aquatic cisticola with **rufous and black upperparts** and buffy underparts. Perches conspicuously on reeds and papyrus while calling a twanging 'chit-chit-chit-tswee'. Never ventures away from marsh vegetation. Sharing the same habitat is the similar **Blackbacked Cisticola** which has a more boldly patterned back and calls 'prrrit-prrrit-prrrit' or a rasping 'zreee'.

Length: 14 cm ss: Blackbacked Cisticola (13 cm)

PS

Cape Reed Warbler

Aquatic warbler with rust-brown back, white underparts and pale eye-stripe. More often heard than seen. Often creeps down reeds to pick insects from water. Call is a melodious warble. Sharing the same habitat are the larger **Greater Swamp Warbler** and the smaller **African Marsh Warbler**; neither has a distinct eye-stripe.

Length: 17 cm ss: Greater Swamp Warbler (18 cm); African Marsh Warbler (13 cm)

BRENDAN RYAN

PS

African Sedge Warbler

Aquatic warbler with **dark brown back**, white underparts and lightly streaked throat and breast. The **long rounded tail** distinguishes it from all other marsh-dwelling warblers. Secretive and seldom seen. The distinctive call – 'cruk-cruk-cruk-cruckcrukcrukcruk' (like a stick being drawn across a railing) – is one of the most familiar sounds of the swamps.

Length: 17 cm

Willow Warbler

Tiny dryland warbler with variable plumage. Most individuals are pale brown above with cream underparts, but others may be grey or pale olive on the back with white or pale yellow underparts. In all cases, a **white eye-stripe and dark line running from bill to eye** are distinctive. Forages for small insects among leaves. Non-breeding **summer migrant** from Europe. Call is a soft melodious song.

Length: 11 cm ss: Icterine Warbler; Garden Warbler

Tawnyflanked Prinia

Tiny, **long-tailed** bird which frequents marshy ground and rank growth near water, but also enters dryland thickets. The **russet wings** and white eye-stripe are distinctive, as is its habit of raising its tail vertically. When disturbed it perches in an exposed position and utters its scolding 'sbee-sbee' call. Also has a 'tritt-tritt-tritt' call.

Length: 14 cm ss: Blackchested Prinia (away from water); Neddicky (11 cm, short tail)

Yellowbreasted Apalis

Tiny, **long-tailed** bird which favours well-wooded habitats. The back is olive, the crown and face are grey and the underparts white with a broad, **lemon-yellow breast**. Males have a small black patch or bar on the chest. Moves rest-lessly among foliage in search of small insects. Usually occurs in pairs, and often joins mixed bird parties. The typical call is an urgent 'chizzick-chizzick-chizzick'.

Length: 13 cm

Yellow White-eye

Tiny, bright yellow bird with lime-green upperparts and distinctive **ring of small white feathers around the eyes**. Occurs in pairs or small flocks in well-wooded areas, foraging for tiny insects among foliage. Also feeds on flower nectar and relishes small berries. Often joins mixed bird parties. The call is a soft 'twee-twee' or a lively warble.

Length: 11 cm ss: Yellowbellied Eremomela (10 cm); Collared Sunbird (see overleaf)

BRENDAN RYAN

73

Collared Sunbird

Tiny, metallic-green sunbird with **bright yellow underparts**. The male has a green throat terminating in a blue and purple band. The bill is much shorter than that of other sunbirds. Occurs in pairs or family groups in tangled vegetation, often joining mixed bird parties. Feeds on small insects and nectar of flowers. Inconspicuous and quiet, the call is a soft 'tswee' or a chirpy song.
Length: 10 cm ss: Yellow White-eye

Whitebellied Sunbird

Tiny sunbird with sexes not alike. The male is **metallic blue-green** on the back and head with a purple-blue throat and **snow-white belly**. The female is grey above, with unstreaked white underparts. The nest is a purse of leaves bound with spider webs. Feeds primarily on the nectar of tubular flowers. Often enters gardens around camps and lodges. Call is a strident tinkling warble.
Length: 11 cm

Marico Sunbird

Small sunbird with the sexes not alike. The male is **metallic green** on the back, head and throat, with a claret breast and **black underparts**. The female is dull brown above and heavily streaked on the throat. Occurs in pairs in all habitats, and frequently seen in the gardens of lodges and camps. Feeds mostly on nectar, but also takes small spiders and insects. Call is a fast swizzling warble.
Length: 14 cm

Scarletchested Sunbird

Medium-sized sunbird with the sexes not alike. The male is uniform dark brown, appearing black, with **bright scarlet chest** with faint blue speckles, and iridescent turquoise forehead and throat. The female is dark brown above and heavily speckled below. Frequently visits gardens of lodges and camps. Feeds mostly on nectar, but also takes spiders and insects. Call is a soft tinkle.
Length: 16 cm ss: Black Sunbird (purple throat)

Swamp Boubou

Medium-sized, black-backed shrike with **snow-white underparts and wing bar**. Occurs in pairs in the dense vegetation of riverine bush and papyrus swamps. Secretive but inquisitive. Call is a variety of liquid or ratchety notes, usually uttered in duet. Feeds on insects. The almost identical **Tropical Boubou** has ivory-cream underparts, and is recorded mostly on the Kwando-Chobe River.
Length: 23 cm ss: Tropical Boubou (23 cm)

Puffback

Small, black-backed shrike with snow-white underparts and white edging to the wing feathers. The eyes are **bright red**. Displaying males erect a puffy mass of white feathers over their back. The female is duller with a white face. Noisy, restless and often confiding. In pairs or mixed bird parties in dense foliage. Feeds on small insects and spiders. The call is a sharp 'tjick-wheeou'.
Length: 18 cm ss: Brubru (15 cm, chestnut flanks)

White Helmetshrike

Medium-sized, black-backed shrike with white underparts and wing bar. The pale grey head is fringed with short, forward-facing plumes. The yellow eyes are ringed by **yellow eye wattles**. Gregarious. Restless flocks of up to 12 fly low from tree to tree, often settling on bare ground. Call is a muffled 'chiroo' – often made in chorus by the group. Feeds on termites, beetles and other insects.
Length: 20 cm

Redbilled Helmetshrike

Medium-sized, all-black shrike with a white vent. The head is fringed with short, forward-facing plumes. The yellow eyes are ringed by **red eye wattles**. The **bill and feet are coral-red**. Gregarious. Restless flocks of up to 12 move through the upper reaches of trees. Occasionally forages alongside the White Helmetshrike. Grating call similar to previous species'. Feeds on caterpillars and insects.
Length: 22 cm

Whitecrowned Shrike

Large, ash-brown shrike with **white crown** and underparts. A dark line runs through the eye to form a **collar on the nape**. Gregarious; small flocks of up to ten perch erect on outer branches of trees, dropping to the ground to capture beetles, other insects and caterpillars. Call is a thin whistle or harsh chatter. Neat, spiderweb-bound nest is often built on an exposed branch.
Length: 25 cm ss: Lesser Grey Shrike (21 cm)

Redbacked Shrike

Small shrike with sexes not alike. The male has a rich **chestnut back**, pale grey head and rump, white underparts and **black mask**. The female is duller on the back, lacks the black mask and is barred on the underparts. Occurs singly in open habitats, perching low on outer branches. Insects are taken on the ground. Silent. Non-breeding **summer migrant**.
Length: 18 cm ss: Threestreaked Tchagra (19 cm); Blackcrowned Tchagra (23 cm)

Orangebreasted Bushshrike

Small shrike with **yellow underparts and eyebrow**, grey head and olive-green wings and tail. The breast is orange. A **black mask** runs through the eye. Pairs keep to tangled undergrowth. Call is a strident, up-tempo whistle – 'whi-whi-whi-whi-wheeo' – or a sequence of harsh alarm notes. Feeds on insects. The larger **Greyheaded Bushshrike** has yellow eyes and lacks the black mask.
Length: 19 cm ss: Greyheaded Bushshrike (27 cm)

Crimsonbreasted Shrike

Medium-sized, black-backed shrike with **crimson underparts** and a white wing bar. Immature is finely barred in grey below with red smudges. Favours semi-arid scrub with acacia thickets, foraging alone or in pairs in lower branches or on ground. Call of the male is a resonant 'quip-quip' with the female adding 'chivi' to the duet; and a snarling 'tjerrr' alarm. Insects are the prey.
Length: 23 cm

Longtailed Shrike

Large, all-black shrike with **long tail**, and white wing bar and tips of the wing feathers. Female is duller with a shorter tail, and white flanks. Gregarious, small flocks of up to ten perch conspicuously in woodland or open areas. Beetles, grasshoppers and other insects are caught on the ground. Call is a squeaky whistle – 'pruuit-preeuo'. Groups are prone to local movements.
Length: 40 to 50 cm

LEX HES

W   S

Redbilled Oxpecker

Dull brown bird with buffy underparts and **bright red bill**. The red eyes are ringed with bare yellow skin. Immature has dark eyes and bill. Gregarious – groups of five or more ride on the backs of large mammals, gathering ticks with a scissormotion of the bill. **Giraffe and antelope** are the favoured hosts. May feed alongside the next species. Group flies off sounding their rasping alarm call.
Length: 22 cm

LEX HES

FG   W   S

Yellowbilled Oxpecker

Dull brown bird with buffy underparts, **pale rump** and **bright yellow bill** tipped in red. The eyes are red. Immature has dark eyes and bill. Gregarious – groups of five or more ride on the backs of large mammals, gathering ticks with a scissor-motion of the bill. **Buffalo and Hippo** are the favoured hosts. May feed along-side the previous species. Group flies off sounding their rasping alarm call.
Length: 22 cm

WILDERNESS SAFARIS/COLIN BELL

FG   W   S

Wattled Starling

Small, cream-buff starling with black wings and tail and distinctive **white rump**. When breeding the male has a bare yellow head adorned with black leathery wattles. Extremely gregarious, occurring in flocks of up to several hundred. Call is a variety of cackles and hisses. Feeds mostly on grasshoppers and prone to nomadic movements. Clustered stick nests are conspicuous.
Length: 21 cm

FG   S

Plumcoloured Starling

Small, iridescent, violet-magenta starling with snow-white belly. Female is distinct, with brown upperparts and white underparts heavily streaked in brown, and yellow gape. Feeds on berries and insects in leafy trees. Occurs in pairs, small groups or flocks of up to 50. Call is a variety of harsh grating notes. **Summer migrant**, breeds in a tree hole. Some individuals may overwinter.

Length: 19 cm

W RF S

Greater Blue-eared Starling

Medium-sized, iridescent, blue-green starling with **pale yellow eyes** and **dark ear patch** behind the eyes. The tail is short. Sexes are alike. Occurs in pairs when breeding, but forms flocks in winter. Call is a nasal 'squerr' – similar to that of the Whitefronted Bee-eater. May become tame around camps and lodges. Breeds in a tree hole. The similar **Glossy Starling** lacks dark ear patches and is darker blue.

Length: 23 cm ss: Glossy Starling (25 cm)

S W

Burchell's Starling

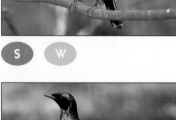

Large, glossy, purple-blue starling with **dark eyes** in a dark mask, and long legs. Duller than the previous species. The tail is broad and kite-shaped. Spends much time on the ground in an upright posture, flying for cover on broad wings. In pairs or small groups, often in the company of hornbills. Beetles, termites and other insects are the main food. Call is a squeaky 'tjerrik'. Breeds in a tree hole.

Length: 34 cm

W S

Longtailed Starling

Medium-sized, glossy blue starling with **dark eyes** but lacking dark mask, and a **long pointed tail**. Perches conspicuously, but comes to the ground regularly to feed on insects. Berries and fruit are also eaten. Occurs in small flocks. Prefers denser woodland to the previous species, being most common in mature Mopane woodland. Call is a series of harsh, chattering notes. Breeds in a tree hole.

Length: 34 cm

W RF

Redbilled Buffalo-weaver

Large weaver. Male is black with **pink bill** and white wing 'windows'. Female is pale ash-brown with a scaly appearance to the breast. Flocks nest communally in a large structure of thorny twigs, set in outer branches of large trees such as a Baobab. Seeds and small insects are eaten on the ground; often in company of starlings. Call is a jumbled chatter. Prone to nomadic movements.
Length: 24 cm

S

Thickbilled Weaver

Dark brown weaver. Breeding male has a **white patch on forehead** and white wing 'windows'. Female is pale brown with mottled back and scaly markings on a pale breast, and has a yellow bill. Occurs in pairs or small colonies in papyrus and reedbeds. The nest is a finely woven structure suspended between two upright stems. Hard seeds are the main food but winged termites are also relished.
Length: 18 cm

PETER HANCOCK

PS   RF

Whitebrowed Sparrow-weaver

Ash-brown weaver with **snow-white underparts, eye-stripe and rump**. The wing feathers are edged in white. Gregarious – small flocks nest colonially in untidy straw nests built in the outer branches of trees. Only one dominant pair breeds in each colony. Favours dry areas with bare ground. Feeds primarily on termites, but seeds are also eaten. Call is a loud liquid song.
Length: 18 cm ss: Yellowthroated Sparrow (15 cm)

S

Greyheaded Sparrow

Chestnut-backed sparrow with **plain grey head**, off-white underparts and narrow white wing bar. The bill is dark when breeding, paler in winter. Occurs in pairs or family groups in well-wooded areas. May form larger flocks in winter. Seeds and small insects are gathered on the ground. Call is a soft 'chirrp-chirrp'. Breeds in a tree hole.
Length: 15 cm ss: Yellowthroated Sparrow (white eyebrow); House Sparrow (confined to towns)

JOHN CARLYON

S

Redshouldered Widow

Medium-sized finch. Male in breeding dress is black with **orange-red shoulders** and pale edges to wing feathers. The bill is ice-blue. Non-breeding males resemble sparrow-like females but retain orange shoulders. Occurs in reedbeds, flood-plains and rank growth along rivers. Displaying males move restlessly from one perch to another. Nest is woven from fine grass. Feeds on seeds and insects.

Length: 19 cm   ss: Whitewinged Widow

Red Bishop

Small finch. Male in breeding dress is **crimson with black face and underbelly**. The bill is black. Females and non-breeding males are drab, sparrow-like and easily overlooked. Occurs in reedbeds and floodplains. Displaying male puffs itself into a ball shape and hangs from reed stem. Call is an excited swizzle. Woven nest is built between upright reeds. Feeds on seeds and insects.

Length: 14 cm

Redbilled Quelea

Small finch. Male in breeding dress has a black mask surrounded by pink or ochre wash, and a **coral-red bill**. Females and non-breeding males are sparrow-like, but also have a red bill. Highly gregarious – flocks of several thousand are common-place. Breeds colonially; woven nests are hung from thorn trees. Raptors, storks and snakes prey on nestlings at noisy colonies. Nomadic.

Length: 13 cm

Redheaded Weaver

Small weaver. Male in breeding dress has a **scarlet head, orange bill**, dusky-olive tail and wings, and white underbelly. Wing feathers are edged in yellow. Female and non-breeding male differ from other weavers in having an **orange bill**. Occurs in pairs or small groups. Woven nest incorporates dry leaves and is suspended from branches or overhead wires. Feeds mostly on insects.

Length: 15 cm

Golden Weaver

Medium-sized yellow weaver with **pale eyes** and stout black bill. Back is olive-yellow. Female is slightly duller than the male which does not assume a dull non-breeding plumage. Woven nest is strung above water. Occurs singly or in pairs, sometimes in mixed bird parties. Call is a prolonged swizzle. Insects, berries and seeds are eaten.

Length: 18 cm ss: Brownthroated Weaver (15 cm); Spectacled Weaver (15 cm)

Masked Weaver

Small weaver. Breeding male is bright yellow below with **red eye in a black mask**. The back is mottled in olive and yellow. Female and non-breeding male are drab olive-yellow. Gregarious – colonies build hanging nests in reedbeds or in trees near water. Call is a noisy, rasping swizzle. Nomadic in winter. The **Lesser Masked Weaver** has pale eyes; **Spotted-backed Weaver** has black spots on back.

Length: 15 cm

Goldenbreasted Bunting

Small, golden-yellow finch with chestnut back and wings. The **head is black with two bold white stripes** above and below the eye. White wing bars are conspicuous in flight. Female is paler yellow below. Usually in pairs, but may form small flocks when not breeding. Occurs in well-wooded habitats, where seeds and small insects are the main food. Call is a lively, nasal song.

Length: 16 cm ss: Rock Bunting (14 cm)

Scalyfeathered Finch

Tiny, grey-brown finch with **pale pink bill** and two distinctive black stripes on the white throat – resembling a beard. The black feathers of the forehead, wing and tail are rimmed in white to give a scaly appearance. Occurs in small flocks in dry acacia scrub. Spends much time on the ground picking up seeds. The nest is a pouch of fine grass.

Length: 10 cm ss: Blackthroated Canary

81

Pintailed Whydah

Tiny finch. Male in breeding dress is black and white with an extremely long, ribbon-like tail of black feathers. The **pink bill** is retained by the non-breeding male which resembles the drab, sparrow-like female. Male usually accompanied by harem of up to six females. Eggs are laid in the nest of the **Common Waxbill**. Favours open habitats, often near water.

Length: 12 cm (plus 22 cm tail in breeding male)
ss: Shafttailed Whydah (ochre underparts)

Paradise Whydah

Tiny finch. Male in breeding dress is black with ochre neck and belly, and rust-red breast. The extravagant tail feathers are broad, tapering at the tips. The bill is black at all times. Females and non-breeding males are drab. Males compete for females in flapping courtship displays on the ground. Eggs are laid in the nest of the **Melba Finch**. Occurs in small flocks of ten or more.

Length: 15 cm (plus 23 cm tail in breeding male)

Redbilled Firefinch

Tiny finch. The male is pale crimson on the face and underparts with a sandy-brown back. A thin yellow ring encircles each dark eye. Female is sandy-brown above with fawn underparts. Both sexes have a pale red bill, **crimson rump** and tiny white spots on the breast and flanks. Feeds on the ground, often with the next species or waxbills, in pairs or small flocks.

Length: 10 cm ss: Jameson's Firefinch (dark bill)

Brown Firefinch

Tiny finch, darker than the previous species. The face and throat of the male is dull crimson. Both sexes have a pale pink bill and a diagnostic **brown rump**. Tiny white spots are clustered on the flanks. Feeds on the ground among leaves often alongside the previous species, but rarely far from water. Occurs in pairs or small flocks, but is inconspicuous.

Length: 10 cm

Melba Finch

Tiny finch. The male is striking with a **scarlet bill, forehead, throat and tail**. The back is olive, head pale grey, and the underparts are finely barred in black and white. The female is duller with no red on the face. Usually occurs in pairs, often in the company of other small seed-eaters. Feeds on the ground. Usual call is a single 'wik' note, but sometimes warbles a lively song.

Length: 12 cm

Blue Waxbill

Tiny finch. The male has a brown back and **powder-blue face, underparts, rump and tail**. The female is paler on the back with a paler blue face and breast, and cream underparts. Occurs in pairs or small flocks in a variety of habits, but most commonly in dry acacia scrub. Feeds on the ground, often in company with other small seed-eaters. Call is a soft but high-pitched whistle.

Length: 13 cm

NATIONAL PARKS BOARD OF S.A.

Violeteared Waxbill

Tiny, long-tailed finch. The male is rich chestnut-brown, with a **bright pink bill** and eye-ring, **violet face**, and **bright blue forehead and rump**. The female is paler overall. Occurs in pairs in dry acacia scrub often in the company of other small seed-eaters, including its brood parasite, the **Shafttailed Whydah**. Usually feeds on the ground. The call is a soft trill.

Length: 15 cm

Common Waxbill

Tiny, grey-brown finch with fine barring on the back and underside. The **bill and mask are rosy-red**, and there is a pink wash over the belly. Sexes are alike, but the immature has a black bill. Occurs in small flocks in reedbeds and in rank growth adjacent to water. Feeds from grass heads rather than on fallen seeds. The call is a jumble of soft tinkling notes.

Length: 13 cm ss: Blackcheeked Waxbill

LEX HES

Reptiles

A wide variety of tortoises, terrapins, snakes and lizards occur in northern Botswana and adjacent Caprivi. Most reptiles are shy, however, and extremely difficult to observe and study in the wild, particularly in the Okavango where walking opportunities are limited. All reptiles are cold-blooded and require food less often than mammals or birds. Many become dormant during cold weather. They are among the most misunderstood and feared of all animals, which is a great pity as most are fascinating and harmless.

Reptiles are usually encountered by chance, but certain species are restricted to particular habitats and may be actively looked for. Many lizards favour open sandy areas, geckos favour walls or tree bark, and terrapins and Water Monitor are common in open water habitats.

Most snakes are nocturnal and seldom seen. Several venomous species occur – some potentially lethal – but they will usually only bite in defence, and then as a last resort. If confronted by a snake, the best strategy is to remain calm and allow it every possible avenue of escape; any attempt to catch or kill it will only increase your chances of being bitten.

The population of the Nile Crocodile is said to be slowly recovering from excessive hunting during the past few decades. It is a most dangerous animal, and swimming in rivers, channels and lagoons is not advisable.

The names used in this section follow those in the *Field Guide to the Snakes and Other Reptiles of Southern Africa* by Bill Branch (Struik, 1988) – the most comprehensive and compact reference book for the region.

Leopard Tortoise

Large tortoise with dull, dome-shaped shell which is neither hinged nor serrated on its rim. Adults weigh between 8 and 12 kg. Moves slowly about a home range of between 1 and 2 km², feeding on plant foliage and berries. Females lay clutches of ping-pong ball-sized eggs in shallow burrows. Young are vulnerable to many predators, and adults to grass fires.
Length: up to 45 cm (max. 72 cm)

Serrated Tortoise

Small tortoise easily identified by the **serrated edge** to its bold, geometrically patterned shell. Typical of dry areas of Kalahari sand, it is most often seen crossing tracks and paths. Fleshy plants and grasses are the main food, but it is also known to eat herbivore droppings. It may retreat into rodent burrows at night. Up to two soft-shelled eggs are laid in a burrow in summer.
Length: 10 to 12 cm ss: Bell's Hinged Tortoise

Okavango Hinged Terrapin

Dark, almost black terrapin with a flat shell and a large **head boldly patterned with yellow streaks**. Occurs in permanent water of rivers, channels and lagoons where it feeds on small fish, frogs and invertebrates. Often seen basking on fallen trunks, and sometimes on the backs of Hippo. The related Marsh Terrapin is paler, has a softer shell and favours temporary pools and pans.
Length: 30 cm ss: Marsh Terrapin (30 cm)

Nile Crocodile

Massive aquatic predator which may live to a great age. Juveniles feed on small animals such as frogs; older crocodiles take large fish and mammals up to the size of antelope. Egg clutches are laid in a sand burrow, and young are guarded by the female. Feared and hated by many humans and valued for its hide; it has been subjected to severe hunting and exploitation in the region.
Length: 3 to 4 m (max. 6 m)

African Rock Python

Huge, thick snake with geometrically patterned skin. Swims well and is fond of swamps. Adults may reach a great size, and are able to capture and swallow prey up to the size of small antelope. All prey is squeezed to death. Although not poisonous, it may inflict a severe ripping bite with its fangs. Most active at dusk and after dark. Up to 50 large eggs are laid in a burrow.
Length: up to 5 m

Brown House Snake

Large, thick-bodied snake which occurs in most habitats, and also in buildings where it preys on rats. The squared-off snout and **two pale lines on either side of the pale eyes** are diagnostic. Body colour is variable, ranging from light brown to rust, becoming darker with age. Prey is killed by constriction, then swallowed head first. Nocturnal. Up to 15 eggs are laid in summer.
Length: up to 1 m (max. 1.5 m)

Common Egg-eater

Small, heavily blotched snake which feeds almost exclusively on birds' eggs. Frequently associated with termite mounds in which it shelters during the day. In a remarkable dietary adaptation, the jaws are able to be dislodged from the neck bones so that eggs, larger than its own head, may be swallowed. Egg-shells are expelled after being sucked of their contents. Up to 25 eggs are laid.
Length: 50 to 70 cm (max. 1 m)

Mopane (Bark) Snake

Small elongated snake with flat head and pointed snout. Lives in the branches of trees, where its mottled, grey-brown skin provides superb camouflage. A dark stripe down the back often forms a zig-zag shape. Small geckos, chameleons and frogs are the main prey, being swallowed while the snake dangles from a branch. Harmless to man, this snake is said never to bite.
Length: 25 to 35 cm

Olive Grass Snake

Fairly large, robust snake; sandy-brown above and pale yellow below. The lip and underside may be finely spotted in black. Occurs in open grassland or scrub but is partial to marshes. Preys on rodents and frogs, but smaller snakes are occasionally eaten. This is a potentially dangerous species which bites readily and injects a painful venom. Primarily nocturnal.
Length: 1 to 1.3 m (max. 1.7 m)

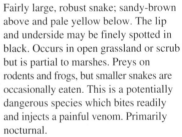

Stripebellied Sand Snake

Slender snake with a beautifully striped body. The background colour is grey or olive, with four cream stripes running down its length. The **white underbelly** is lined by a yellow stripe edged in black. Occurs mostly in dry open habitats, climbing into low bushes at times. Prey consists mostly of rodents and lizards. Bites readily if handled. Active by day.
Length: up to 1 m

Spotted Bush Snake

Slender snake varying from dull olive to bright emerald in colour, with black spots and bars. The head is rather flat in shape. Active by day, it moves swiftly through and up trees in search of small geckos, chameleons and tree frogs. When agitated or threatened, it may inflate its neck to reveal bright blue skin, and strike out. Lacking fangs and venom glands, it is harmless to man.
Length: up to 1 m

Western Green Snake

Slender snake varying in colour from olive- to emerald-green and sometimes with scattered, pale blue spots. The belly is pale green. The **black skin between the scales** is diagnostic. Active by day, it forages in moist grassland or reedbeds, rarely, if ever, climbing trees. Frogs and nestling birds are the main prey. When threatened, the neck is inflated to reveal black skin. Harmless, but bites readily.
Length: up to 1 m

Boomslang (Tree Snake) ☠

Fairly large thin snake characterised by big eyes. It is variable in colour. Males are bright or dull green with some black and pale blue markings. Females are pale olive-brown. Juveniles are greyish with a white chin, yellow throat and green eyes. Active by day, it feeds mostly on birds and chameleons. Shy, but extremely dangerous if handled – the venom may prove fatal to man.
Length: 1 to 2 m

Vine (Twig) Snake ☠

Slender snake with a distinctive **pointed head** and **red tongue with black tip**. The skin is intricately patterned and serves as superb camouflage. Active by day, it waits in ambush for chameleons, geckos and small birds. Prey is swallowed as the snake dangles off a branch. Unless handled, bites are improbable, but the venom is highly toxic and potentially fatal to humans.
Length: up to 1m

87

Eastern Tiger Snake

Small slender snake. The body varies from orange to salmon-pink with numerous transverse dark bands on the back. Active only at night, it scales dead trees to search crevices and holes for roosting birds, bats and lizards. Prefers dry, open habitats, including semi-desert. Slow-moving. Aggressive, it is said to bite readily, but the venom is mild and harmless to man.

Length: 55 to 80 cm

Mozambique Spitting Cobra

Fairly large, thick-bodied snake. Forages on the ground, preying mostly upon rodents and toads. When threatened it rears up and spreads its hood; it may then eject venom into the eyes of an adversary. The colour varies from olive-brown to pale grey, with a pinkish belly and black throat. Mostly active after dark. Often takes up residence under buildings.

Length: up to 1.5 m

Black Mamba

Large sleek snake with a coffin-shaped head and permanent 'smile' caused by the wide mouth. Body colour varies from dusky-olive to ash-grey, but is never black. Feeds mostly on birds and small mammals. Strongly territorial. Greatly feared, but will readily retreat if allowed to do so. If cornered it will strike repeatedly and even a small dose of venom is usually fatal to man.

Length: 2 to 3 m (max. 4.3 m)

Puff Adder

Short stocky snake, boldly patterned in ochre, tan and black. The scales are keeled, giving a rough appearance and texture. Although most active at dusk and after dark, it may be seen during the day. Rodents, frogs and ground birds are the main prey. Litters consist of 20 to 40 young. It is sluggish and will bite readily, usually below the knee. The venom is potentially fatal to man.

Length: 70 to 90 cm (max. 1.2 m)

Striped Skink

Small, dark, shiny lizard, with a long tapered tail. Active by day, it **keeps mostly to trees**, but is found in a wide variety of habitats. It often lives around buildings. Beetles and other insect prey are captured after a chase. Young are born live, and do not hatch from eggs. The closely related **Variegated Skink** is pale sandy-grey with darker speckles on the back, and rarely climbs trees.
Length: 18 to 20 cm

LEX HES

Common Roughscaled Lizard

Medium-sized lizard with a **long tail, and overlapping scales on the back**. Active by day, it keeps to the ground, feeding mostly on termites and small grasshoppers. Adults are fawn on the back with dark crossbands and six rows of small spots. Burrows are excavated in loose sand at the base of small trees. The similar **Bushveld Lizard** is smooth-scaled.
Length: 16 to 20 cm

Rock Monitor

Massive, **dry-land** lizard with a **rounded snout**. Often **climbs trees**. Adults are grey-brown on the back with pale blotches, and pale yellow below with dark spots and bands. Juveniles are more brightly coloured. Feeds on anything it can over-power, and also scavenges. Up to 30 soft-shelled eggs are laid – usually in a self-excavated hole. The Martial Eagle is its main predator.
Length: up to 1 m

Water Monitor

Massive **aquatic** lizard with an **elongated snout**. Adults are dark olive-brown or grey-brown on the back, and paler below. Juveniles are patterned in yellow and black. Feeds on anything it can over-power, including crabs, frogs, and the eggs of crocodiles and birds. Females lay 20 to 60 soft-shelled eggs in a hole in an active termite mound. The strong tail is used in defence.
Length: 1 to 2 m

WILDERNESS SAFARIS/COLIN BELL

89

Ground Agama

Plump, ground-dwelling lizard with a large **triangular head** and ridges around the eyes. Common in dry open habitats. The male is conspicuous during summer when it sits in exposed sites, showing blue sides to its head. In this position, it often bobs up an down in a territorial display. Eggs are laid in sandy soil. Feeds on ants, termites and other small insects. Usually wary.
Length: 15 to 22 cm

Moreau's Tropical House Gecko

Chubby, **nocturnal** gecko which lives under the bark of trees, but often takes up residence in buildings where it hunts moths and other insects around lights. The scales on the flat toes have minute hairs which allow it to cling to smooth surfaces. The body is pale grey to pink-brown with darker bars. Males may fight vigorously and often lose their tail tips. A single tiny egg is 'glued' into a crevice.
Length: 12 to 16 cm

Cape Dwarf Gecko

Tiny gecko, which is **active by day**. It lives on the trunks and branches of trees, but can be common on the outdoor walls of buildings. Termites, ants and other insects are the prey. Males are territorial. A pair of tiny, hard-shelled eggs are laid in cracks or crevices. The related Chobe Dwarf Gecko is virtually identical, but keeps mostly to the upper branches of trees.
Length: 6 to 7 cm ss: Chobe Dwarf Gecko (8 cm)

Flapnecked Chameleon

Distinctive reptile with big rounded head and **conical eyes**. The tail is often curled up. Adults are usually green, but are able to change colour to match foliage, bark or soil. Slow-moving, it is **active by day**. Most conspicuous when on the move after rain. A clutch of 25 to 50 eggs is buried in soil. Flies and other insects are caught with the long sticky tongue. Snakes are the main predators.
Length: 20 to 24 cm

Frogs

The wetlands of the Okavango Delta abound in frogs, some of which may be among the most numerous of animals on the floodplains and waterways. Not all frogs depend upon permanent water, however, as many species are adapted to dry habitats and emerge only after rain to breed in temporary pans.

Frogs have two stages in life: the tadpole (larval) which is usually totally aquatic, and the four-limbed adult which may be active in and out of water. Many species exhibit unusual breeding behaviour.

Like birds, frogs have distinctive calls and this facilitates their identification and study. Most species are only active after dark, however, and are best found by going out at night with a strong torch after, or during, rain. This is, of course, not advisable in the Okavango region where many potentially dangerous nocturnal animals are present. Several frog species are likely to occur in the vicinity of private camps and lodges and it may be possible to arrange for a guide to accompany you on a 'frogging' walk. Remember that snakes have as much interest in frogs as any naturalist. Some species of frog, including the toads, enter rooms and tents to hunt insects and may seek refuge inside shoes (as will numerous other creatures); it is wise to shake your shoes out before putting them on in the morning!

The names used in this section follow those in *South African Frogs* (Southern and Wits Univ. Press, 1995) by Neville Passmore and Vincent Carruthers. This book includes most of Botswana's frog species. A cassette tape entitled *Voices of South African Frogs* supplements this work.

Common Platanna

Extraordinary frog with a compressed body and **eyes on the top of its head**. Usually seen suspended just below the water surface. It is almost totally aquatic, but may move about during rain. The fore limbs are short and slender, but the hind legs are large and powerful with webbing between the **clawed toes**. Preys upon small fish, insects and tadpoles, and will also scavenge. Said to call underwater.
Length: 5 to 8 cm ss: Tropical Platanna

VINCENT CARRUTHERS

O

Giant Bullfrog

Huge, olive-green frog with orange armpits and yellow throat. Adults bite if handled. Remains underground in winter, but numbers emerge after heavy summer rains to occupy temporary pans. The adults fight, mate and produce large numbers of eggs which develop rapidly before the water dries up. Preys upon other frogs and rodents. The call is a deep 'whoop'.
Length: 8 to 20 cm

VINCENT CARRUTHERS

FG S

Banded Rubber Frog

Medium-sized, rather flat frog. The body is mostly black in colour with broad bands of red, pink or yellow on the back, and small spots on the legs. These warning colours advise would-be predators of its unpalatability; the skin is said to exude toxins. Most frequent in rain-filled pans and on floodplains. Males sit at the water's edge and call with a loud, repetitive trill.
Length: 5 to 6 cm

Mottled Shovelnosed Frog

Small, mole-like frog with a squat, swollen body and a pointed snout. The back is sandy-brown with dark grey blotches and the underside is pinkish-white. Occurs in open habitats near pans and pools on floodplains. Males call with a repetitive buzz from shallow burrows at the water's edge. The snout is used as a shovel to burrow underground, where the jelly-coated eggs are laid.
Length: 3 to 4 cm

Guttural Toad

Mottled, sandy-brown or grey toad with a **pair of dark patches on the snout**, and red, blood-like flecks on the thighs. It breeds in permanent water but often forages some distance away and is often seen around outdoor lights after dark. The call is a reverberating snore often uttered in chorus by numerous males at the water's edge. Begins calling in early spring. May gather in groups to feed on termites.
Length: 5 to 7 cm

Olive Toad

Mottled, sandy-brown or grey toad with an **unmarked snout**. Like the Guttural Toad it may have red flecks on the thighs. It breeds in temporary pans and marshes in savanna or woodland. The call is a loud bray, repeated at one second intervals by groups of males from **exposed positions** at the water's edge. Breeding is rain stimulated. May gather in groups to feed on termites.
Length: 5 to 7 cm

Foamnest Frog

Medium-sized frog with slender, webbed toes tipped with adhesive pads. It lives in the branches of trees but frequently enters buildings. The body colour is variable in shades of grey or tan, but when sitting in sunlight the skin turns a chalky white. The eggs are laid in a foamy nest – whipped-up by the mating couple and a gaggle of unpaired males – hung from a branch over water.
Length: 5 to 6 cm

Bushveld Rain Frog

Tiny rotund frog with a down-turned mouth which gives it a permanently grumpy appearance. The back is mottled in various shades of brown, tan and buff, and the underparts are white. It spends most of its life underground in a torpid state, emerging (often in large numbers) after rain. Eggs are laid underground, and the tadpoles live in moist chambers until they change into froglets.
Length: 3 to 4 cm

Sharpnosed Grass Frog

Small streamlined frog with powerful hind legs and pointed snout. The **back is olive-brown with dark blotches** and bars; the underside is white. Up to six raised ridges run down the back. Although frequently abundant on floodplains and in marshes, it is secretive and easily overlooked. The call is a high-pitched trill or shriek. Difficult to catch as it constantly leaps out of reach.
Length: 5 to 6 cm ss: Broadbanded Grass Frog

Mascarene Grass Frog

Small streamlined frog with powerful hind legs and pointed snout. The **back is plain greenish-brown**; the underside is cream. The **groin is green**. Up to six raised ridges run down the back. Although it may be abundant on floodplains and in marshes, it is secretive and easily over-looked. The call is a nasal bray followed by a series of clicks. Difficult to catch as it constantly leaps out of reach.
Length: 4 to 5 cm ss: Dwarf Grass Frog (3 to 4 cm)

93

VINCENT CARRUTHERS

Painted Reed Frog

Tiny, brightly coloured frog. Adults are **variable in colour**, with white bodies streaked, spotted or blotched in red and black; juveniles are olive-fawn. Flattened discs on the toe tips enable it to climb on slippery surfaces; it often clambers into boats. Abundant in reedbeds and flooded grassland on the edges of lagoons and pans. The call is a monotonous, short whistle. Many males call simultaneously.
Length: 3 cm

VINCENT CARRUTHERS

PS FG

Long Reed Frog

Tiny frog with **sharply pointed snout**. The long legs and flattened discs on the toe tips enable it to climb on slippery surfaces. The body is translucent green or olive-brown, with two white stripes down the flanks. Common in flooded grassland and on the edges of lagoons and pans. The call is an acute chirp, repeated every few seconds. Many males call simultaneously.
Length: 2 cm

VINCENT CARRUTHERS

Bubbling Kassina

Small, boldly patterned frog. The back is variable in colour, being fawn, yellow or olive, but the bold dark stripes are distinctive. The sides are mottled and the underbelly off-white. It is most common on floodplain grasslands but is seldom seen due to its retiring habits. The call is a loud liquid 'quoip', made from the base of a grass tuft, often well away from water.
Length: 5 to 6 cm

VINCENT CARRUTHERS

Common Caco

Tiny squat frog which is only active after rain. The body colour is extremely variable, ranging from emerald-green to dull brown. Stripes, blotches and spots may be present. If caught, the **white underbelly with dark spots** is diagnostic. Numbers gather at temporary pans and pools to breed, calling monotonously at night and on cloudy days. Secretive, and difficult to find.
Length: 2 cm ss: Snoring Puddle Frog

Freshwater Fishes

The Okavango Delta supports a great diversity of fishes, with over 60 species having been recorded. An additional 12 or more species are known from the upper reaches of the Okavango River and the Kwando-Chobe System. Only 18 of the more common or interesting species are featured here.

Fish are traditionally of more interest to anglers than they are to naturalists, but there is much to be marvelled at in their appearance, behaviour and ecology. Time spent with a rod or net should yield several species for observation, and these can be released thereafter. For keen anglers, the Okavango is one of Africa's premier destinations, with large Tigerfish, Nembwe, Redbreasted Tilapia and African Pike being most sought after. Permission to catch fish may be obtained from private camps and lodges. Fish of many kinds are the most important source of protein for the local people.

There are numerous threats to the fish fauna of the Okavango. Paramount among these is the ongoing spraying of insecticides to combat the spread of tsetse fly. Fish may be poisoned by these chemicals and they are also indirectly affected by the poisoning of invertebrates leading to a depletion of food resources. Of great concern is the spread of alien aquatic plants such as Kariba Weed *Salvinia molesta* (p. 120) which diminishes light and oxygen levels.

Names used in this section follow those in *A Complete Guide to the Freshwater Fishes of Southern Africa* by Paul Skelton (Southern, 1993). This is the most comprehensive and easy-to-use guide to the 245 indigenous and introduced freshwater fishes of southern Africa.

Western Bottlenose

Fairly large, elongated fish with a long, proboscis-like snout. The dorsal fin is extended to near the tail. Prefers quiet stretches of water with emergent vegetation. Active mostly at night, feeding primarily on insect larvae and snails. May occur in small shoals. Research has shown that they are able to communicate with weak electronic pulses. Frequently caught by fishermen.
Length: 50 cm

PAUL SKELTON

Bulldog

Medium-sized, compressed fish with a bulbous lower jaw, which protrudes beyond the upper. The dorsal and anal fins are set far back on the body. It lives in shoals, being most common in the shallow waters of floodplains. Insect larvae, including mosquitoes, are the main food. This fish forms a major part of the diet of the Sharptooth Catfish during the annual 'catfish run' in early summer.
Length: 30 cm ss: Churchill

PAUL SKELTON

Dashtail Barb

Small, finger-sized fish which belongs to one of the largest fish genera in Africa – *Barbus*, the minnows or barbs. The body is silvery-white to olive-brown above, and paler below. A single **black oblong spot** occurs at the base of the tail. Some individuals have two or more 'shadow' spots. Lives in shoals in clear water, often in floodplain shallows. Numerous closely related species occur.
Length: 10 cm

Striped Robber

Small, finger-sized fish, similar in appearance to the Dashtail Barb, but unrelated. Mimicry has been suggested between these species, but the reasons for this are not clear. A single **black spot** occurs at the base of the tail, but is **edged in yellow**. A second dorsal fin is set above the tail. Occurs in shoals, often in company with barbs, in clear, well-vegetated waters.
Length: 14 cm

Johnston's Topminnow

Tiny elongated fish with a yellowish-green back and pale underside. Iridescent, silvery-blue scales are often present on the sides and gill covers. Differs from the barbs in having the single dorsal fin set well back. The small **mouth points upward**. Lives in small shoals among vegetation in shallow water. Vulnerable to kingfishers and fishing spiders.
Length: 5 cm ss: Striped Topminnow

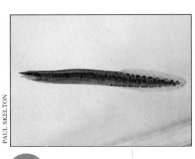

Longtailed Spiny Eel

Medium-sized, eel-like fish with an acutely pointed snout and the dorsal fin modified and extended into a row of well-spaced spines. The body is pale brown with speckles. Occurs in fringing vegetation of channels and rivers, where it preys mostly on insects. Spiny Eels differ from true eels in that their life-cycle does not involve sea-spawning (no eels are present in the Okavango).
Length: 30 cm ss: Ocellated Spiny Eel

Tigerfish

Large silvery fish with distinctive **parallel black stripes** on the flanks. The fins are pointed and strikingly coloured in yellow or red. Sharply pointed teeth protrude from the strong jaws. Preys mostly upon small shoaling fish. Occurs in rivers and larger lagoons, keeping mostly to the upper surface. Often taken by African Fish Eagle. Aggressive and fierce, it is a prized angling fish.
Length: 70 cm (female); 50 cm (male)

African Pike

Medium-sized, elongated fish with a **pointed head**. Sharp, uneven teeth protrude from the jaws. The fins are not pointed. Overall colour is shiny olive-brown with darker blotches and spots. Three dark streaks radiate back from the eye. Occurs singly or in pairs in deep water of channels and lagoons, where it ambushes and eats fish up to half its own size. A prized angling species.
Length: 47 cm (female); 40 cm (male)

Banded Jewelfish

Fairly small, brightly coloured fish also known as the Jewel Cichlid. Typical of the cichlid family, the long dorsal fin is spine-tipped in its front half and soft-rayed at the rear. Pairs are strongly bonded and guard their 'nest' and developing brood (unlike most other cichlids, they do not hold their young in the mouth). Lives in permanent, clear water, preying on shrimps and insects.
Length: 15 to 20 cm

Southern Mouthbrooder

Small, brightly coloured fish belonging to the large cichlid family. Males are usually yellow, or iridescent light blue, with the front (spiny) part of the dorsal fin red. All fins are speckled in blue. Females are pale brown. Males establish and defend a territory, and build a simple nest; females brood eggs, larvae and juveniles, taking them into the mouth. Prefers clear, vegetated water.
Length: 13 cm

PAUL SKELTON

Nembwe

Fairly large, thick-set fish; olive to bright green with a dark band along the body. The largemouths (or serranos) – of which this is one of six species present in the Okavango – are predatory cichlids distinguished by their large, strongly upturned mouths. The Nembwe prefers lagoons and channels, where it hunts smaller fish. The eggs and young are mouth brooded. Prized angling fish.
Length: 45 cm ss: Thinface Largemouth

PAUL SKELTON

Banded Tilapia

Small, oval-shaped fish varying in colour from olive to bronze, with darker bars and blotches. A dark 'tilapia spot' is conspicuous at the base of the soft dorsal fin. Breeding males have the dorsal fin rimmed in red. Algae, plants, insects and even small fish are eaten. Pairs are strongly bonded, with both sexes guarding the brood of eggs and young. They do not take young into the mouth.
Length: 23 cm ss: Okavango Tilapia (10 cm)

PAUL SKELTON

Redbreasted Tilapia

Fairly large fish, mostly olive brown with five to seven vertical bars on the flanks. The **throat and chest are red**. The end of the extended dorsal fin is pointed, tipped in yellow or red. Occurs in a wide variety of habitats, but prefers floodplains. Waterlily leaves are the main food. The distinctive, bowl-shaped nests may be seen in shallow water. Popular angling species, and a tasty 'table fish'.
Length: 40 cm

PAUL SKELTON

Threespot Tilapia

Fairly large, blue-grey fish with pale scale edges creating a wire mesh appearance. Three dark, but usually faint, spots occur on each flank. Breeding males have the dorsal and tail fins rimmed in crimson. Favours slow-moving or standing water of floodplain pans and lagoons. Detritus and tiny organisms are the main food. A fine angling fish.
Length: 45 cm

Manyspined Climbing Perch

Small elongated fish with spines on the edge of the gill covers and on the dorsal and anal fins. The body is bronze-brown, with darker blotches and spots; dark bands radiate back from the eye. Occurs mostly in shallow water habitats, including floodplains and lagoons, feeding on small invertebrates. Remarkable, air-breathing organs (above the gills) allow it to move over land in wet weather.
Length: 13 cm

PAUL SKELTON

Silver Catfish (Butter Barbel)

Medium-sized fish with an elongated, kite-shaped body and flattened head. The colour ranges from silvery-grey to pale olive. Unlike other catfishes, which are bottom-dwellers, this species forages in mid-water. In common with its relatives, it lacks scales and has thin tendrils (barbels) on its mouth. The dorsal and anal fins are spine-tipped. Fair eating, but a nuisance to most anglers.
Length: 30 cm

PAUL SKELTON

Sharptooth Catfish (Barbel)

Large, scaleless fish with compressed body, bony head and filament-like tendrils (barbels). Slate-grey above, white below. Fish of this *Clarias* genus are unique in being able to breath air. Favours flood-plains where it feeds on a variety of food. Hunts in packs during the annual 'catfish run' – upstream in early summer. Popular angling and food fish. Numbers may become trapped in evaporating pools.
Length: up to 1.4 m ss: Blunttooth Catfish

R A JUBB

Finetooth Squeaker

Small, scaleless fish with a triangular shape when seen head on. The body is pale tawny-yellow and covered with numerous dark spots or bars. The dorsal fin is large and has a **sharp spine** which can be 'locked' to act as a weapon. If taken out of the water it lets out a grunt or squeak. Feeds on detritus. The family is well represented in the Okavango region, with six similar species.
Length: 30 cm

PAUL SKELTON

Invertebrates

The animal kingdom is divided into two broad groupings. The 'higher' classes, from fishes to mammals, are typified by an internal skeleton and are known as *vertebrates*. The 'lower' classes lack an internal skelton, are generally much smaller in size, and are known as *invertebrates*. There is an enormous number of different invertebrates and new species are constantly being identified and named.

Due to the presence of so many impressive mammals and birds, most visitors to the Okavango Delta and surrounding areas pay scant attention to invertebrates. But no matter how small they may be, some will soon be noticed if only for their painful bite or incessant noise.

Once synonymous with the Okavango, the tsetse fly has been championed by conservationists as Africa's 'finest game warden' – this blood-sucking insect transmits sleeping sickness to cattle and, until large-scale spraying with insecticides was initiated in the 1960s, kept man and his stock from much of Africa's wilderness regions. It is now virtually extinct in the Okavango. Mosquitoes are abundant and some species carry malaria, for which medication should be taken before entering the area. Blood-sucking leeches are common in still water and may attach themselves to feet and lower legs.

Despite their small size, many invertebrates are fascinating subjects to observe and they often allow a more intimate examination of their lives than do larger animals. Sitting quietly at the edge of a lagoon, or exploring vegetation in the vicinity of camps, will reveal many interesting insects, spiders and other invertebrates. A small magnifying glass (8x or 10x is ideal) and a glass jar for temporarily housing specimens will aid study. Insects and other invertebrates make excellent photographic subjects, but a macro lens is essential.

Only a few of the more interesting, irritating or noticeable invertebrates are featured here and all – except the colourful butterflies and moths – are identified to family level only.

A list of more detailed publications relating to invertebrates is provided on p. 122. *Butterflies of Southern Africa – A Field Guide* by Mark Williams (Southern, 1994), is an easy-to-use guide to over 200 butterfly species.

LEX HES

Water snails

Small aquatic molluscs with soft bodies. A brittle shell is secreted, growing in size with age, and is used as a mobile retreat. Feed mostly on algae on reed stems and under waterlily leaves.

Leeches

Small segmented worms with flattened mouth parts used for attachment to host – usually fish – from which it sucks blood. Dark in colour. Most common in still water such as at inlets of islands.

PETER LAWSON

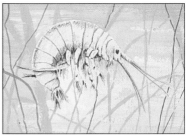

River crabs

With large pincers and sideways walk, these crabs are unmistakable. They occur in all permanent water habitats, but may travel over land after rain. Feed on insects, tadpoles, small fish and carrion.

Freshwater shrimps

Tiny, delicately built shrimps with almost transparent, pinkish bodies and very long antennae. Most abundant in the permanent swamp where they live among papyrus roots. Feed on detritus.

NATIONAL PARKS BOARD OF S.A.

LEX HES

Millipedes

Long cylindrical arthropods with hair-like legs. Movement is slow, but they are avoided by most predators as they eject a pungent, toxic fluid. Curl into a spiral if threatened. Usually black.

Ticks

Small, eight-legged relatives of spiders. They become engorged after feeding on the blood of larger animals. May transmit diseases such as tick-bite fever. Should be looked for on skin after walks.

LEX HES

AS SCHOEMAN

Scorpions

Eight-legged arachnids with large pincers and sting-tipped tail curved over the body. Prey on insects. Most species are nocturnal. Species with small pincers and fat tails have the most toxic venom.

Solifuges

Eight-legged arachnids with large jaws, but no long tail. Prey on spiders and insects. Most species are nocturnal, often approaching campfires. Although fearsome-looking, they are not poisonous.

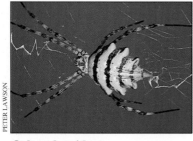

Orb-web spiders

Large, usually yellow and black spiders which construct hanging webs to trap prey. The webs of some are golden in colour, and strong enough to hold small birds. Male is tiny compared to female.

Fish-eating spiders

Long-legged spiders which occur in vegetation alongside water. No webs are made. Small fish, as well as reed frogs and tadpoles, are ambushed and dragged out of the water to be eaten.

Jumping spiders

Small, ground-living spiders with large obvious eyes. No web is made. Small insects such as flies and ants are pounced upon after a stalk. Some species mimic ants in colour and shape.

Baboon spiders

Very large spiders, incorrectly referred to as tarantulas by some. Large body and long hairy legs are distinctive. No web is made. Prey, mostly large insects, is ambushed. Eggs are laid underground.

Damselflies

Small delicate insects usually associated with open water. Unlike the similar dragonflies, the wings are held above the body when at rest. Small insects are caught in flight. Larvae develop in water.

Dragonflies

Small to large insects always associated with open water. Over 60 species in the Delta, many brightly coloured. Wings are held at right angles to the body when at rest. Predator. Larvae develop in water.

PETER LAWSON

JAMES MARSHALL

Praying mantids

Predatory insects with distinctive enlarged forelimbs used to capture flies and beetles. Well camouflaged in shades of green or pink. Females larger than males. Often feeds around lights.

Stick insects

Large insects, so well camouflaged that they are only noticeable when on the move. The small wings are brightly coloured and are held upright when threatened. Predators of small insects.

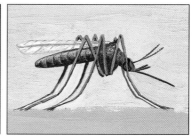

Pond skaters

Tiny, slender aquatic bugs which 'skate' across the surface of the water. Usually occur in colonies, noticeable by ripples on the water. Prey mostly upon drowning insects.

Mosquitoes

Tiny, fly-like insects. Only the females suck blood and make the irritating whining noise. Males are silent and feed on plant sap. Eggs are laid in still water. Some species transmit malaria.

LEX HES

Cicadas

Cryptically coloured bugs which are rarely seen due to their remarkable camouflage. Males make an incessant and shrill noise on hot summer days and evenings. All are sap suckers.

Dung beetles

Distinctive beetles with extremely powerful hind limbs and a flat shield on the snout. Adults are attracted to animal dung, rolling balls away backwards. Eggs are laid in dung balls.

103

Termites

Tiny herbivorous insects with a complex social order. Colonies consist of a 'queen', sterile workers, sterile soldiers and winged reproductives (alates) which emerge after rain. Most build mounds.

Ants

Tiny gregarious insects which are usually black or red in colour. Colonies consist of a 'queen', workers and soldiers. Most are carnivorous, but some feed on sap or 'honeydew' secreted by aphids.

Grasshoppers

Herbivorous insects with powerful hind legs held in an inverted V-shape above the cigar-shaped body. Several species are brightly coloured. Locusts are migratory, swarm-forming grasshoppers.

Honey bees

Small gregarious insects which feed on nectar and are attracted in large numbers to flowering plants. Complex social order, with a colony building a hive in a tree hole. Sting is potentially dangerous.

Blow flies

Small flies, usually metallic-blue or green with orange eyes. Feed on carrion, around which they may gather in large swarms. Adults may also lay eggs in the flesh of living animals.

Tsetse flies

Distinguished by wings which fold on top of one another, the bite of these flies is painful and may cause sleeping sickness in cattle and man. Most have been eliminated by the spraying of pesticides.

Lunar Moth

A spectacular, pale green moth with extended 'tails' on the lower wings. In common with all moths the antennae are feathered. This is a nocturnal, nectar-feeding species, as are most other moths.

Mopane Emperor Moth (larva)

Colourful caterpillar known as a 'Mopane Worm', which is the larva of a drab, pale brown moth. Feeds exclusively on the foliage of Mopane trees. Relished by many bird species and also by man.

African Monarch

Rust-red butterfly with wings marked in black and white. In common with all butterflies, it is active by day and has thin clubbed antennae. Body fluid is toxic, so it is avoided by predators.

African Migrant

Males are white above with pale green underwings; females are lemon-yellow above with tan wing tips, and mottled yellow below. May form large mirgatory flocks. Often drinks from puddles.

Whitebarred Charaxes

Large, fast-flying butterfly which usually perches high in trees but comes to ground to drink from puddles or suck fluid from carnivore dung. Upperside of wings less boldly marked than the underside.

Brownveined White

Small, predominantly white butterfly with brown patterns on the wings; females have a yellow wash. Large numbers migrate in flocks at the middle or end of summer.

Trees and Woody Shrubs

In comparison to the eastern parts of southern Africa, the diversity of trees in the Okavango Delta region is relatively small. Nevertheless, most of the best-known bushveld trees are found here, often reaching proportions greater than elsewhere. Magnificent specimens of Umbrellathorn, Sausage Tree, Jackalberry and Sycamore Fig occur in abundance, while tall woodlands of Mopane and Zambezi Teak cover extensive areas. This section features 50 of the more conspicuous or common trees and woody shrubs.

The identification of trees and shrubs is considered a daunting prospect by beginners, but one way of getting to know them is to actively **look for the species featured here**. Exploring the area around campsites and lodges is a good way of getting to know trees as bark, leaves, flowers and fruits are within reach. A number of more detailed books of trees and shrubs are available, and these are listed on p. 122. The standard reference book is *Trees of Southern Africa* by Keith Coates Palgrave (Struik, 1977), but *The Shell Field Guide to Common Trees of the Okavango Delta and Moremi Game Reserve* by Veronica Roodt (Shell, 1993) is a useful publication specific to the Okavango Delta.

In this section, the scientific names of the trees are given before the common names. It is important to learn and use these names, as any future study of trees will involve regular comparison between related species and common names are often misleading in this regard. Except where the shape of the tree is so unique as to be diagnostic – such as the Baobab and Fan Palm – the photographs illustrate only the leaves, and where possible flowers and fruit.

Phoenix reclinata
Wild Date Palm/Tsaro

Bushy palm with **dark green, feather-shaped leaves** up to 4 m long. Forms clumps in damp situations and is the dominant plant on the outer fringes of islands. Also grows on termite mounds. Clusters of creamy-white flowers are held in orange sheaths. Edible fruits appear in late summer; yellow ripening to brown.

ARECACEAE Height: 3 to 8 m

Hyphaene petersiana
Fan (Ivory) Palm/Mokolwane

Tall palm with **grey-green, fan-shaped leaves** up to 1.2 m wide. Usually forms colonies on islands and floodplains, and is one of the few trees which can grow on saline soils. Impenetrable, spiny thickets often grow beneath mature trees. Small flowers appear in early summer. Large round fruits hang on the tree throughout the year and are eaten by elephant; the ivory-like core is used for curios.

ARECACEAE Height: up to 20 m

Ficus sycomorus
Sycamore Fig/Mochaba

Massive spreading tree with smooth, pale
yellow trunk and branches. Usually
grows near water. Leaves simple, rough;
in spirals around stems. Contains milky
latex. Evergreen. Large figs green, ripening to orange; borne on branchlets off
main stems throughout the year. Birds,
bats, monkeys, fish and insects among
many animals which eat the figs.

MORACEAE Height: up to 30 m

BETH PETERSON/AFRICAN IMAGES

Ficus burkei (thonningii)
Common Wild Fig/Moumo

Large spreading tree with smooth, pale
grey bark on a fluted trunk. Often has
aerial roots hanging from branches and
is **frequently a strangler of other trees**.
Leaves simple, glossy with long petiole;
in spirals around stems. Contains milky
latex. Evergreen. Small stalkless figs are
massed along stems; relished by birds
and bats.

MORACEAE Height: up to 15 m

Ficus verruculosa
Water Fig/Gomoti

Small bushy tree restricted to water-
logged areas, and common on fringes of
channels and lagoons. Storks and other
birds nest in thickets. Trunk pale grey.
Leaves simple, glossy, dark green above,
paler below with warty spots, short petiole; in spirals around stems. Contains
milky latex. Evergreen. Small figs at
base of leaves; ripening to red.

MORACEAE Height: 1 to 3 m

Boscia albitrunca
Shepherd's Tree/Motopi

Stout tree with pale bark being rough
and yellowish or smooth and almost
white. Leaves are small, simple, leathery,
dull grey-green, oblong; in spirals
around stems. Heavy browsing by
antelope often results in a flat base to the
crown. Small greenish flowers in clusters
in early summer. Yellow berries ripen to
red in midsummer.

CAPPARACEAE Height: 3 to 9 m

PIET VAN WYK

Albizia harveyi
Sickleleaved Albizia/Molalakgaka

Tall tree with spreading crown and bare trunk. Widespread. Closely resembles acacias, but **lacks thorns**. Bark grey with vertical ridges. Leaves bipinnately compound with tiny, sickle-shaped leaflets. Cream, powder-puff flowers in clusters, early summer. Pods thin, flat, russet-brown, up to 15 cm; split in late summer to release seeds. Deciduous.
MIMOSACEAE Height: up to 15 m

Acacia erioloba
Camelthorn/Mogotlho

Tall tree with spreading crown and bare trunk. Widespread on sandy soils. Bark dark brown with deep ridges. Leaves bipinnately compound with small oval leaflets. Thorns straight. Bright yellow, ball-shaped flowers in summer; sweet scented. **Pods fat, velvety, pale grey**; do not split, but are eaten by many animals, which then spread seed. Deciduous.
MIMOSACEAE Height: up to 17 m

Acacia hebeclada
Candlepod Acacia/Setshe

Small tree with dense, tangled crown. Occurs on poorly drained soils. Pendant branches create hideaways for carnivores. Bark grey with vertical grooves. Leaves bipinnately compound with tiny oval leaflets. Thorns hook-shaped. Cream, ball-shaped flowers in summer. Pods **broad, smooth, grey-fawn and pointing upwards like a candle**. Deciduous.
MIMOSACEAE Height: 5 m

Acacia nigrescens
Knobthorn/Mokoba

Tall, upright tree with rounded crown. Abundant on silty alluvial soils (not sand) on the fringes of floodplains. Bark is rough and bears large, thorn-tipped knobs. Leaves bipinnately compound with **leaflets larger than in any other acacia**. Thorns hook-shaped. Spikes of cream flowers cover the tree in spring. Pods are thin, papery. Deciduous.
MIMOSACEAE Height: 15 to 25 m

Acacia tortilis
Umbrellathorn/Moshu

Impressive, flat-topped tree with dense
crown and bare, low-branching trunk.
Widespread on clayey, alluvial soils. Bark
is grey and vertically grooved, much
favoured by Elephant. Leaves bipinnately
compound with tiny leaflets. Thorns are
straight and white **and** hook-shaped.
Flowers are cream balls in early summer.
Pods coiled in clusters. Deciduous.
MIMOSACEAE Height: up to 15 m

Acacia sieberiana
Paperbark Acacia/Morumosetlha

Large, flat-topped tree with sparse crown
and bare, low-branching trunk. Widespread
on sandy, alluvial soils. Bark is corky,
pale yellow; peels off in papery sections.
Leaves bipinnately compound with tiny
leaflets. Thorns straight, white. Flowers
are creamy-white balls during summer.
Pods large, broad, smooth, pale sandy-
brown. Deciduous.
MIMOSACEAE Height: up to 12 m

Dichrostachys cinerea
Sicklebush/Moselesele

Small tree or shrub with acacia-like
appearance. Usually multi-stemmed,
often forms thickets. Widespread on
sandy soils. Bark is grey-brown, deeply
grooved. Leaves bipinnately compound
with tiny leaflets. Thorns straight, dark
brown. Flowers are pretty, pink and
yellow catkins during summer. Pods are
twisted in bunches. Deciduous.
MIMOSACEAE Height: up to 5 m

Burkea africana
Wild Syringa/Mosheshe

Tall, flat-topped tree with sparse crown
and long bare trunk. Widespread on
Kalahari sands to the west and north of
the Delta. Bark is dark grey, rough and
divided into small blocks. Leaves pale
blue-green, bipinnately compound with
terminal leaflets off-centre. No thorns.
Tiny flowers are fragrant. Pods are flat,
single-seeded capsules. Deciduous.
CAESALPINIACEAE Height: up to 15 m

Colophospermum mopane
Mopane/Mophane

Large, often V-shaped tree with rounded crown. Abundant and dominant on poorly drained clay soils, as tall single-species woodland or low scrub. Bark is grey and deeply furrowed. Leaves are simple, split into a butterfly shape; bright green when young, ageing to coppery-red. Flowers inconspicuous. Fruit is a thin, kidney-shaped pod. Deciduous.
CAESALPINIACEAE Height: up to 18 m

JOHN BURROWS

Baikiaea plurijuga
Zambezi Teak

Tall tree with dense, spreading crown. Typical of deep Kalahari sand away from floodwaters, where it dominates woodland. Bark is furrowed. Leaves compound with four or five pairs of oval leaflets; no terminal leaflet. Flowers attractive, pink-mauve in summer. Pods are velvety, paddle-shaped, hooked tip; split to release seeds. Deciduous.
CAESALPINIACEAE Height: up to 16 m

Piliostigma thonningii
Camelfoot/Segagama

Bushy tree with weeping shape. Prefers sandy soil. Bark is grey-brown, rough and furrowed. Large leaves simple, alternate, deeply notched and leathery. Flowers small, pale yellow in terminal sprays in late summer. Fruit is a large woody pod – up to 22 cm – which does not split but is eaten by monkeys and baboons. Deciduous.
CAESALPINIACEAE Height: up to 6 m

Pterocarpus angolensis
Kiaat/Morotomadi

Tall tree with sparse, spreading crown of drooping leaves. Occurs on Kalahari sand or among rocks; most common in Caprivi. Bark dark, furrowed. Exudes a blood red sap. Leaves compound with terminal leaflet. Small yellow flowers in bunches, midsummer. Fruit is a distinctive round pod, with papery fringe and spiky centre.
FABACEAE Height: up to 16 m

Lonchocarpus capassa
Rain Tree/Mopororo

Tall, **irregularly shaped** tree with twisted trunk and sparse foliage. Reaches greatest size on floodplain margins. Bark is pale grey-brown, flaking off in blocks. Leaves compound, with one or two pairs of leaflets and terminal leaflet; frequently eaten by insects. Flowers small, lilac, pea-shaped in early summer. Pods thin, papery, in clusters. Deciduous.
FABACEAE Height: up to 20 m

Phyllanthus reticulatus
Potato Bush

Scrambling shrub or small tree, common in riverine woodland. Easily overlooked, but the pervasive scent of cooked potato, given off by the small flowers in the evening, is a characteristic smell of the Okavango. Small leaves are simple and alternate. Tiny flowers are inconspicuous. Small round berries hang in clusters. Partially deciduous.
EUPHORBIACEAE Height: 2 to 10 m

Croton megalobotrys
Large Feverberry/Motsebi

Rounded bushy tree with dense, drooping foliage. Occurs on alluvial soils, with young plants forming dense undergrowth. Bark is smooth, pale grey. Leaves simple, alternate, heart-shaped with serrated margin. Small cream flowers are inconspicuous in terminal bunches. Fruit is a small, three-lobed woody capsule. Partially deciduous.
EUPHORBIACEAE Height: up to 15 m

Schinziophyton rautanenii
Manketti /Mongongo

Large spreading tree restricted to dry Kalahari sand; most common in Caprivi. Trunk is often swollen. Bark smooth, pale grey or fawn, peeling. Stems exude milky latex. Leaves digitately compound with five to seven oval leaflets; dark green above, pale below. Yellow flowers hang in sprays in early summer. Fruit is a velvety, egg-shaped capsule. Deciduous.
EUPHORBIACEAE Height: up to 20 m

PIET VAN WYK

111

Sclerocarya birrea
Marula/Morula

Large tree with a spreading crown. Bark is pale grey, peeling off in disc-shaped flakes. Leaves compound with three to seven pairs of oval leaflets and terminal leaflet; long petioles and pointed tips. Flowers tiny. Yellow fruits ripen on ground in summer; relished by Elephant, Chacma Baboon and people. Deciduous; bare branches and stems point upwards.
ANACARDIACEAE Height: up to 20 m

Maytenus senegalensis
Confetti Tree/Mothono

Scruffy, multi-stemmed shrub or small tree often forming thickets. Branches and stems armed with sharply pointed spines. Leaves simple, alternate or in clusters, leathery, blue-green with scalloped margin and blunt tip. Flowers borne in profusion in midwinter; creamy-white. Fruit is a small, two-lobed capsule. Evergreen.
CELASTRACEAE Height: up to 4 m

Ziziphus mucronata
Buffalothorn/Mokgalo

A small crooked tree with low-branching trunk and untidy appearance. Widespread. Stems grow in zig-zag fashion and are armed with paired thorns – one straight, one hooked. Bark is grey, flaking off in vertical strips. Leaves simple, alternate, finely toothed, glossy; markedly three-veined from base. Flowers small. Fruit a hard, red-brown, edible berry. Deciduous.
RHAMNACEAE Height: 3 to 10 m

Berchemia discolor
Brown Ivory/Motsintsila

Large impressive tree with a dense rounded crown. Widespread. Bark is rough, grey-brown with furrows and blocks. Leaves are simple, opposite or alternate, oval, with distinct **'herring-bone' veins** on paler undersurface. Flowers inconspicuous in clusters. Fruit is a small fleshy berry, green ripening to red, relished by birds and man. Deciduous.
RHAMNACEAE Height: up to 20 m

112

Adansonia digitata
Baobab/Mowana

Gigantic squat tree which may live for thousands of years. Unmistakable when leafless in winter. The bark is smooth and fibrous, and is much favoured by Elephant. The leaves are palmate with five oval leaflets. Flowers are large and showy, opening mostly at night and pollinated by bats. Seeds are in white pulp within a large velvety pod.
BOMBACACEAE Height: up to 25 m

Garcinia livingstonei
African Mangosteen/Motsaodi

Medium to large evergreen tree with **dark green foliage**, and **angular stems and branches**. Exudes yellow sap. Most common near water, particularly on islands in the Delta. Leaves are thick, stiff and glossy; borne in threes at stem tips. Flowers are insignificant, but the edible, orange, plum-like fruits are conspicuous in midsummer.
CLUSIACEAE Height: up to 18 m

Syzygium cordatum
Waterberry/Mokowa

Medium-sized, evergreen tree with a crooked shape which grows adjacent to permanent water. Frequent along channels and island fringes. The oval leaves are leathery, in opposite pairs, and clasp the stem with the **petiole short or absent**. White flowers consist mostly of stamens. Edible fruits are purple when ripe. The related *S. guineense* has longer petioles.
MYRTACEAE Height: up to 15 m

Diospyros mespiliformis
Jackalberry/Motutshumo

Large impressive tree which reaches greatest size along watercourses, but is also frequent on termite mounds. The bark is dark and textured. Simple leaves are alternate, oval, shiny, and usually have wavy margins. Flowers are tiny pale yellow bells. Round berries ripen to yellow and are fed upon by birds, antelope, baboons, squirrels, and – it is said – by jackals. Deciduous.
EBENACEAE Height: up to 25 m

113

Combretum imberbe
Leadwood/Motswiri

Large deciduous tree with a straight trunk and sparse crown. Leaves are small, grey-green and in pairs on **spiny stems**. Bark is pale grey, with the texture of elephant skin. Small, four-winged **pods are pale yellow**. The wood is hard and heavy and this tree is said to live for thousands of years. Dead specimens may remain standing for centuries.
COMBRETACEAE Height: up to 20 m

Combretum hereroense
Russet Bushwillow/Mokabe

Small deciduous tree with crooked branches often trailing close to the ground. Leaves are small, dark green above and paler below, in pairs. Bark is variable in colour, flaky in older trees. Small, four-winged **pods are russet-red** and cover the whole tree in summer. Flowers inconspicuous. Often grows in association with Mopane on clay soils.
COMBRETACEAE Height: up to 8 m

Combretum mossambicense
Knobbly Combretum/Motsheketsane

Shrub or scrambling creeper most common on the fringes of floodplains and on termite mounds. Leaves are fairly large, oval and opposite, or nearly so. The bark is grey-brown and smooth. Small **pods are usually five-winged**. The showy white flowers have **orange anthers**; sweetly scented, they appear in profusion in spring. Deciduous.
COMBRETACEAE Height: up to 4 m

Combretum celastroides
Jessebush Combretum

Dense untidy shrub or small tree prone to form thickets in dry woodland and most common on Kalahari sand. Oval leaves are smooth, sparsely hairy; in opposite pairs. Small, four-winged **pods have distinctive reddish 'wings'** when fresh, but dry to a golden-brown. Creamy-white flowers lack the orange anthers of *C. mossambicense* and are in sparse clusters. Deciduous.
COMBRETACEAE Height: up to 4 m

114

Terminalia prunioides
Purplepod Terminalia/Motsiara

Dense, tangled shrub or small tree which usually grows in shallow, poorly drained soils. The small, dark green leaves have a squared-off tip; in clusters. The bark is grey and furrowed, and the wood heavy and hard. White flowers are borne in dense spikes in summer. Bright purple pods may cover the tree throughout the winter. Deciduous.

COMBRETACEAE Height: up to 8 m

Terminalia sericea
Silver Terminalia/Mogonono

Tall graceful tree with distinctive, silvery-grey foliage. Typically grows in deep sands, or in the 'seep-line' where clay and sandy soils meet. Bark is dark and deeply furrowed. Leaves are borne in clusters. Flowers are in spikes and have a pungent scent. Pods are pale pink. Branchlets are often covered in swollen galls caused by larvae of small insects.

COMBRETACEAE Height: up to 18 m

Kigelia africana
Sausage Tree/Moporoto

Large deciduous tree with a short squat trunk. Most frequent along river banks or the fringes of islands. The compound leaves have up to four pairs of leaflets and terminal leaflet; crusty in texture. Bark is pale grey and smooth. Flowers are spectacularly pipe-shaped with crinkly crimson petals. The extraordinary fruits are up to a metre long.

BIGNONIACEAE Height: up to 20 m

Trichilia emetica
Natal Mahogany/Mosiki

Large evergreen tree with a dense rounded crown. Always occurs in the vicinity of water. The trunk is usually low-branching and covered in scaly bark. The compound leaves consist of up to eleven leaflets; dark green and very glossy above, paler and hairy below. Small greenish flowers are inconspicuous. Spherical fruits split to reveal orange-red seeds.

MELIACEAE Height: up to 20 m

115

Capparis tomentosa
Woolly Caperbush/ Motawana
Scrambling climber or small evergreen tree. Small hooked thorns grow in the axils of the velvety leaves. **Ball-shaped fruits have long stalks**.
CAPPARACEAE Height: up to 8 m

Carissa edulis
Climbing Numnum/Simboba
Scrambling shrub armed with paired spines. Leathery leaves have pointed tips. Flowers are white, star-shaped. Oval fruits purple. Exudes milky latex.
APOCYNACEAE Height: up to 3 m

Ximenia caffra
Large Sourplum/ Morotonoga
Shrub or small evergreen tree growing in a variety of habitats. Leaves are leathery and dark green. Stems spiny. Fruit is bright red; edible but extremely sour.
OLACACEAE Height: up to 4 m

Grewia flava
Brandybush/Moretlwa
Small shrub typical of dry woodland on Kalahari sand. The oval leaves are grey-green above, much paler below. Star-shaped flowers and berries are yellow.
TILIACEAE Height: up to 2 m

Diospyros lycioides
Red Star Apple/Letlhajwa
Small shrub or slender tree growing in a variety of habitats. Soft, oval leaves are clustered on stems. Red, marble-sized **berries have star-like bracts**.
EBENACEAE Height: up to 3 m

Euclea divinorum
Magic Guarri/Mothakola
Dense evergreen shrub typical of poorly drained soils. Slender **leaves are shiny with wavy margins**. Frayed twig ends can be used as a toothbrush.
EBENACEAE Height: up to 5 m

Bauhinia petersiana
White Bauhinia/Mogutswe
Spreading shrub typical of sandy soil.
Leaves are distinctively two-lobed.
Attractive, crinkly white flowers. Long
pods contain beans used to make 'coffee'.
CAESALPINIACEAE Height: up to 3 m

Baphia massaiensis
Sand Camwood
Sparsely foliaged shrub typical of
Kalahari sand; associated with Zambezi
Teak. White, jasmine-scented flowers
appear in summer. Pods are narrow.
FABACEAE Height: up to 5 m

Vernonia amygdalina
Tree Vernonia/ Moqune
A dense shrub or small tree common on
the margin of floodplains. Leaves are
oblong with pointed tips. Clustered
flower heads appear in winter.
ASTERACEAE Height: up to 5 m

Gardenia volkensii
Savanna Gardenia/Morala
Small thickset tree. Leaves are leathery,
and borne in threes at stem tips. Flowers
are showy white with waxy petals. The
fruit is a ribbed drupe.
RUBIACEAE Height: up to 8 m

Kirkia accuminata
White Syringa/Modumela
Medium-sized tree restricted to rocky
outcrops. Compound leaves have 6 to 10
pairs of lance-shaped leaflets; foliage
turns coppery-red in autumn.
SIMAROUBACEAE Height: up to 15 m

Croton gratissimus
Lavendar Feverberry/Omumbango
Slender tree with drooping shape; most
common on rocky outcrops. The small
oval leaves are shiny green above, white
below with small, orange-brown spots.
EUPHORBIACEAE Height: up to 8 m

Soft-stemmed Shrubs and Herbs

A wealth of small herbaceous plants occur in the Okavango Delta region, but this short section introduces only a few of the most conspicuous. Space limitations demand that many common plants have had to be left out. Particular attention has been given to aquatic and semi-aquatic plants as these are obvious when boating through the Delta. Many of these plants grow in dense, single-species communities.

The identification of smaller plants is often a complex matter and is usually carried out with the help of an identification key. Such an approach is not possible within the confines of this guide. As is the case with trees, one way of becoming familiar with the species featured here is to actively look for them – they will not be difficult to find.

Among the other small flowering plants which it has not been possible to feature here, are various species of *Ipomoea, Cleome, Plumbago, Pluchea,* and *Clerodendrum.*

Asclepias fruticosa ☠
Milkweed/ Mositanokana
Sparsely foliaged shrub typical of disturbed soils. Leaves are lance-shaped. All parts exude a poisonous **milky latex**. Seeds are in an inflated hairy capsule.
ASCLEPIADACEAE Height: up to 2 m

Leonotis nepetifolia
Wild Dagga
Erect, sparsely branched herb with soft, serrated leaves. The tubular orange flowers are set at widely spaced intervals on the stems; much favoured by sunbirds.
LAMIACEAE Height: up to 2 m

Abrus precatorius ☠
Luckybean Creeper
Twining climber with small compound leaves and lilac pea-shaped flowers. Triangular pods split to reveal shiny red and black seeds.
FABACEAE Height: up to 2 m

Dissotis canescens
Wild Tibouchina
Upright herb typical of marshy places. Stems and oval leaves are hairy. The pink, star-shaped flowers are most prolific in summer and autumn.
MELASTOMATACEAE Height: up to 1.5 m

Nymphaea nouchali caerulea
Day Waterlily
Commonest waterlily in the region, often forming dense mats on still water. Flowers open by day – white at first, pink after pollination. Leaf margins entire.

NYMPHAEACEAE

Nymphaea lotus
Night Waterlily
Less common than the previous species. The **creamy-white flowers have yellow anthers**; open at night and close as the sun rises. **Leaves have toothed margins**.

NYMPHAEACEAE

Nymphoides indica
Water Gentian
Small floating herb with heart-shaped leaves. Often grows in association with waterlilies. Star-shaped flowers have hairy petals; white (rarely yellow).

MENYANTHACEAE

Trapa natans
Water Chestnut
Floating herb, typical of the fringes of channels and lagoons. Triangular, toothed leaves rimmed in red; petioles red and swollen. Fruit is a horned capsule.

TRAPACEAE

Brasenia schreberi
Water Shield
Free-floating herb with small, oval, waterlily-like leaves. Stems and leaves are covered with a **clear slimy gel**. Stems and small flowers are red.

CABOMBACEAE

Ottelia ulvifolia
Water Lettuce
Aquatic herb with trailing underwater stems and broad leaves. The plant is rooted, rather than free-floating. Most common in slow-flowing channels.

HYDROCHARITACEAE

Salvinia molesta *
Kariba Weed

Free-floating fern native to tropical America. **Invasive alien** which smothers surfaces. Subject of erradication programmes in the Delta and elsewhere.

SALVINIACEAE

Eichhornia crassipes *
Water Hyacinth

Free-floating herb native to tropical America. **Invasive alien** which smothers surfaces. Occurs in the Chobe River and must be watched for in the Delta.

PONTEDERIACEAE

Sansevieria aethiopica
Mother-in-law's Tongue

Low-growing perennial which often forms small colonies. The leaves are fibrous, speckled, sharp-edged and pointed. Favours clay soils.

DRACAENACEAE

Drosera madagascariensis
Sundew

Tiny insectivorous plant of marshy places. The fleshy, spoon-shaped leaves are rimmed with sticky hairs which entrap mosquitoes and other insects.

DROSERACEAE

Thelypterus interrupta
Swamp Fern/Letetemetsu

Aquatic fern which grows in dense communities on the fringes of channels and lagoons. Fronds may reach 1 m in length.

THELYPTERIDACEAE

Typha capensis
Bulrush

Grass-like perennial which forms dense stands in shallow water. Rarely exceeds 2 m in height. The flowers are packed on a distinctive velvety spike.

TYPHACEAE

120

Grasses and Sedges

Grasses play a vital role in the ecology of ecosystems, particularly in Africa where they support large numbers of grazing herbivores. Sedges are related to grasses, differing mostly in the shape of their flower heads and being primarily aquatic.

Among the common grasses which it has not been possible to feature are *Cymbopogon excavatus* Turpentine Grass, *Panicum maximum* Guinea Grass, *Setaria sphacelata* Bristle Grass, and *Imperata cylindrica* Cottonwool Grass.

Cyperus papyrus
Papyrus/Koma
Tall graceful sedge, this is the dominant plant of permanent swamp. Grows in extensive, dense colonies. Source of the world's first paper. Leafless.

CYPERACEAE Height: up to 2.5 m

Phragmites australis
Common Reed/Lethaka
Tall reed typical of permanent swamp. Prefers shallower water than Papyrus, but the two may grow side by side. Leaves are razor sharp.

POACEAE Height: up to 2 m

Miscanthus junceus
Miscanthus Grass/Moxaa
Robust perennial grass associated with swamp, but preferring more elevated ground than Papyrus or Common Reed. Quill-like leaves have sharp tips.

POACEAE Height: up to 2 m

Sporobolus spicatus
Spike Grass/Tshunga
Creeping perennial grass with a low, lawn-like growth. Leaves have sharp, **needle-like tips**. Largely restricted to white powdery 'soils' (trona) on islands.

POACEAE

Cynodon dactylon
Couch Grass/Mutwa
Creeping perennial grass with a low, lawn-like growth. Typical of flood-plains. Important grazing grass and able to withstand trampling.

POACEAE

121

REFERENCES AND FURTHER READING

GENERAL

McCarthy, T.S. 1992. Physical and biological processes controlling the Okavango Delta – a review of recent research. *Botswana Notes and Records*, 24: 57-86.

Ross, K. 1987. *Okavango: Jewel of the Kalahari.* Southern Books, Halfway House & BBC Books, London.

Stuart, C. & T. 1994. *Field Guide to the Tracks and Signs of Southern and East African Wildlife.* Southern Books, Halfway House.

Tinley, K.L. 1973. *An Ecological Reconnaissance of the Moremi Wildlife Reserve, Northern Okavango Swamps, Botswana.* Okavango Wildlife Society, Johannesburg.

Walker, C. 1991. *Savuti: The Vanishing River.* Southern Books, Halfway House.

GEOLOGY

Pritchard, J.M. 1986. *Landscape and Landform in Africa.* Edward Arnold, London.

MAMMALS

Apps, P. 1992. *Wild Ways: Field Guide to the Behaviour of Southern African Mammals.* Southern Books, Halfway House.

Estes, R.D. 1995 *Behaviour Guide to African Mammals.* Russel Friedman Books, Halfway House.

Skinner, J.D. & Smithers, R.H.N. 1990. *The Mammals of the Southern African Subregion* (2nd edition). University of Pretoria, Pretoria.

Stuart, C. & T. 1988. *Field Guide to the Mammals of Southern Africa.* Struik, Cape Town.

BIRDS

Chittenden, H. 1992. *Top Birding Spots of Southern Africa.* Southern Books, Halfway House.

Gibbon, G. 1991. *Southern African Bird Sounds* (set of 6 cassettes). SA Birding cc, Durban.

Ginn, P.J., McIlleron, W.G. & Milstein, P. le S. 1989. *The Complete Book of Southern African Birds.* Struik Winchester, Cape Town.

MacLean, G.L. (Ed.) 1993. *Roberts' Birds of Southern Africa* (6th edition). John Voelcker Bird Book Fund, Cape Town.

Newman, K. 1989. *Birds of Botswana.* Southern Books, Halfway House.

Newman, K. 1992. *Birds of Southern Africa* (4th edition). Southern Books, Halfway House.

Penry, H. 1994. *Bird Atlas of Botswana.* Natal University Press, Durban.

Sinclair, I., Hayman, P. & Arlott, N. 1993. *Sasol Birds of Southern Africa.* Struik, Cape Town.

REPTILES

Branch, B. 1988. *Field Guide to the Snakes and Other Reptiles of Southern Africa.* Struik, Cape Town.

Broadley, D.G. 1983. *Fitzsimons' Snakes of Southern Africa.* Delta Books, Johannesburg.

FROGS

Passmore, N.I. & Carruthers, V.C. 1995. *South African Frogs* (2nd edition). Southern Books, Halfway House &Wits. Univ. Press, Johannesburg.

FRESHWATER FISHES

Skelton, P.H. 1993. *A Complete Guide to the Freshwater Fishes of Southern Africa.* Southern Books, Halfway House.

INVERTEBRATES

Filmer, M. 1991. *Southern African Spiders: An Identification Guide.* Struik, Cape Town.

Migdoll, I. 1987. *Field Guide: Butterflies of Southern Africa.* Struik, Cape Town.

Pinhey, E.C.G. 1975. *Moths of Southern Africa.* Tafelberg, Cape Town.

Pringle, E.L.L., Henning, G.A. & Ball, J.B. (Eds.) 1994. *Pennington's Butterflies of Southern Africa* (2nd edition). Struik, Cape Town.

Skaife, S.H. (revised by J.A. Ledger) 1979. *African Insect Life.* Struik, Cape Town.

Williams, M. 1994. *Butterflies of Southern Africa: A Field Guide.* Southern Books, Halfway House.

PLANTS

Coates Palgrave, K. 1983. *Trees of Southern Africa.* Struik, Cape Town.

Ellery, K. & W.N. *A Field Guide to the Plants of the Okavango Delta, including Moremi Game Reserve.* (In press.)

Ellery, W.N., Ellery, K., Rogers, K.H., McCarthy, T.S. & Walker, B. 1990. Vegetation of channels of the north-eastern Okavango Delta, Botswana. *African Journal of Ecology*, 28: 276-290.

Roodt, V. 1993. *The Shell Field Guide to the Common Trees of the Okavango Delta and Moremi Game Reserve.* Shell, Gaborone.

PICTORIAL

Aiken, B. 1986. *Lions and Elephants of the Chobe.* Struik, Cape Town.

Forrester, B., Murray-Hudson, M. & Cherry, L. 1989. *The Swamp Book.* Southern Books, Halfway House.

Johnson, P., Bannister, A. & Bond, C. 1977. *Okavango: Sea of Land, Land of Water.* Struik, Cape Town.

Lanting, F. 1993. *Okavango: Africa's Last Eden.* Russel Friedman Books, Halfway House.

Potgieter, H. & Walker, C. 1989. *Okavango from the Air.* Struik, Cape Town.

CONSERVATION

Scudder, T. *et al.* 1992. *The IUCN Review of the Southern Okavango Integrated Water Development Project.* Draft Final Report, Gaborone.

Williamson, D.L. 1994. *Botswana – Environmental Policies and Practices Under Scrutiny: The Lomba Archives.* Ntsu Foundation, Parklands.

TRAVEL

Comley, P. & Meyer, S. 1994. *Traveller's Guide to Botswana.* New Holland, London.

Main, M. & Fowkes, J. 1994. *Visitors' Guide to Botswana.* Southern Books, Halfway House.

DESTINATIONS AND USEFUL ADDRESSES

TOUR OPERATORS

Okavango Wilderness Safaris
P/Bag 14, Maun, Botswana. Tel.
660 632. (Reservations in South Africa:
Wilderness Safaris. Tel. (011) 884 1458)

Afro Ventures Safaris
PO Box 2339, Randburg, 2125,
South Africa. Tel. (011) 789 1078

Karibu Safaris
P/ Bag 39, Maun, Botswana.
Tel. 660 493

Peter Comley Safaris
PO Box 55, Kasane, Botswana.
Tel. 650 234

Namib Wilderness Safaris
PO Box 6850, Windhoek, Namibia.
Tel. (061) 226 178/4

CAMPS AND LODGES

Central Okavango Delta
**Jedibe Island Camp; Mombo
Camp; Tchau; Pompom; Xaxaba;
Delta Camp; Gunn's Camp;
Oddball's Camp; Shindi Camp;
Camp Okavango; Xugana Lodge**

Eastern Okavango Delta
**Machaba Camp; Khwai River
Lodge; Tsaro Lodge; Okuti;
Camp Moremi; Santawani Lodge**

Pan-Handle/Okavango River
**Xaro Lodge; Fish Eagle Lodge;
Shakawe Fishing Camp; Guma
Camp; Nxamaseri**

Savuti/Linyanti
**Lloyd's Camp; Savuti South;
Linyanti Camp; Selinda Camp**

Chobe River
**Chobe Game Lodge; Kubu Camp;
Chobe Chilwero; Cresta Mowana**

East Caprivi
Lianshulu Lodge (on the Kwando
River, Mudumu National Park);
Impalila Island Lodge (confluence
of Zambezi and Chobe rivers);
Kalizo Lodge (Zambezi River)

PUBLIC CAMP SITES

Moremi Game Reserve
Maqwee Camping Site (South Gate);
Khwai Camping Site (North Gate);
Third Bridge Camping Site;
Xakanaxa Camping Site

Chobe National Park
Savuti Camping Site (Savuti plain);
Serondela Camping Site (Chobe
River); Noghatsau Camping Site

GOVERNMENT AGENCIES

**Botswana Department of
Wildlife and National Parks**
P/Bag 131, Gaborone, Botswana.
Tel. (267) 371 405

**Namibian Ministry of Wildlife,
Conservation and Tourism**
P/Bag 13346, Windhoek 9000,
Namibia. Tel. (061) 220 241

CONSERVATION

**Kalahari Conservation
Society – Okavango Branch**
P/Bag 28, Maun, Botswana

**Kalahari Conservation
Society – Head Office**
PO Box 859, Gaborone, Botswana
Tel. (267) 374 557

Okavango Wildlife Society
PO Box 52362, Saxonwold 2132,
South Africa Tel. (011) 880 3833

Wildlife Society Namibia
PO Box 3508, Windhoek, Namibia

EDUCATIONAL

Botswana Society
PO Box 71, Gaborone, Botswana

National Museum Botswana
PO Box 71, Gaborone, Botswana

State Museum Namibia
PO Box 1203, Windhoek, Namibia

BIRDS

Botswana Bird Club
PO Box 71, Gaborone, Botswana

Namibian Bird Club
PO Box 67, Windhoek, Namibia

FRESHWATER FISHES

**J.L.B. Smith Institute of
Ichthyology**
P/Bag 1015, Grahamstown, 6140,
South Africa. Tel. (0461) 27124

GLOSSARY OF SCIENTIFIC TERMS

alien – an organism introduced by
man, and now naturalised in a
region or country in which it does
not belong

aquatic – living in water

arboreal – living in trees

alluvial – deposit of soil or sand
left by flood

alternate – leaves which are
arranged singly at different points
on a stem

anal – rear end, anus

anther – pollen-bearing part of a
flower

axil – upper joint between a leaf
and a stem

bipinnate – a compound leaf in
which the leaflets are further
divided into pinna (eg *Acacia*)

bract – leaf-like structure from
which a flower arises

calcrete – white laterite rock rich
in calcium

compound – a leaf consisting of
several leaflets (eg *Kigelia*)

crepuscular – active at twilight, or
just before dawn

deciduous – a plant which sheds
its leaves at the end of the growing
season

dorsal – upper surface of the body

dorsal fin – fin on the spine of a
fish

drupe – a fleshy, non-splitting fruit

epiphyte – an organism that grows
on another but is not parasitic

food chain – the sequence
whereby plants are consumed by
herbivorous animals which are then
preyed upon by other animals.

gills – breathing organs of fishes

herbivorous – eating plant matter

indigenous – an organism occurring naturally in an area

latex – a white, sticky liquid

leaflet – divided leaf

mimic – one animal resembling
the form or colour of another, in
order to obtain some benefit

naturalised – an organism which
has been introduced from elsewhere
and is reproducing successfully in a
new area

native – *see* indigenous

opposite – leaves which are
arranged opposite to one another
on a stem

parasite – an organism which
obtains its food from another
organism (host)

perennial plant – a plant which
lives for at least three years

perennial river – a river which
flows throughout the year

petiole – leaf stalk

pinna – divided part of a leaflet

pinnate – a compound leaf divided
into leaflets

roost - nighttime resting place of
birds or bats

simple leaf – an undivided leaf

scale – a thin, plate-like structure

scalloped – leaf margin notched
with blunt projections

spike – an elongated stem which
bears more than one flower

serrated – margin notched with
fine projections

terminal – at the end of a stem

terrestrial – living on the ground

toothed – leaf margin notched
with pointed projections

trifoliate – a leaf which is divided
into three leaflets

ventral – undersurface

whorled the arrangement of
three or more leaves or flowers at
the same point on a stem to form
an encircling ring

INDEX OF FEATURED SPECIES

MAMMALS

Baboon, Chacma — 29
Bat, Cape Serotine — 33
Bat, Common Slitfaced — 33
Bat, Little Freetailed — 33
Bat, Peters' Epauletted Fruit — 32
Bat, Yellow House — 33
Buffalo — 21
Bushbaby, Lesser — 29
Bushbuck — 23
Cane Rat, Greater — 30
Cheetah — 25
Civet — 27
Dormouse, Woodland — 31
Duiker, Common — 24
Elephant, African — 20
Elephant Shrew, Shortsnouted — 32
Fox, Bateared — 27
Fruit Bat, Peters' Epauletted — 32
Genet, Largespotted — 27
Genet, Smallspotted — 27
Gerbil, Bushveld — 31
Giraffe — 21
Hare, Scrub — 30
Honey Badger — 27
Hippopotamus — 20
Hyena, Spotted — 26
Impala — 23
Jackal, Blackbacked — 26
Jackal, Sidestriped — 26
Kudu, Greater — 23
Lechwe, Red — 22
Leopard — 25
Lion — 25
Mongoose, Banded — 28
Mongoose, Dwarf — 28
Mongoose, Marsh — 28
Mongoose, Water — 28
Monkey, Vervet — 29
Mouse, Singlestriped — 31
Mouse, Tree — 31
Musk Shrew, Lesser Red — 32
Night Ape — 29
Otter, Cape Clawless — 28
Otter, Spottednecked — 28
Porcupine — 32
Puku — 22
Ratel — 27
Reedbuck, Common — 22
Sable Antelope — 22
Serval — 25
Sitatunga — 23
Springhare — 30
Squirrel, Tree — 29
Steenbok — 24
Tsessebe — 24
Vlei Rat, Angoni — 30
Warthog — 21
Waterbuck, Common — 22
Wild Dog — 26
Wildebeest, Blue — 24
Zebra, Burchell's — 21

BIRDS

Apalis, Yellowbreasted — 73
Babbler, Arrowmarked — 67
Babbler, Hartlaub's — 67
Babbler, Pied — 67
Babbler, Whiterumped — 67
Barbet, Blackcollared — 63
Barbet, Crested — 63
Bateleur — 49
Batis, Chinspot — 71
Bee-eater, Bluecheeked — 60
Bee-eater, Carmine — 61
Bee-eater, European — 60
Bee-eater, Little — 60
Bee-eater, Swallowtailed — 60
Bee-eater, Whitefronted — 61
Bishop, Red — 80
Boubou, Swamp — 75
Boubou, Tropical — 75
Buffalo-weaver, Redbilled — 79
Bulbul, Blackeyed — 67
Bulbul, Yellowbellied — 66
Bunting, Goldenbreasted — 81
Bushshrike, Greyheaded — 76
Bushshrike, Orangebreasted — 76
Bustard, Kori — 53
Chat, Arnot's — 69
Chat, Stone — 70
Cisticola, Blackbacked — 72
Cisticola, Chirping — 72
Cisticola, Rattling — 72
Cisticola, Tinkling — 72
Cormorant, Reed — 35
Coucal, Copperytailed — 56
Coucal, Senegal — 56
Crake, Black — 44
Crane, Wattled — 41
Crombec, Longbilled — 71
Crow, Pied — 65
Cuckoo, Diederik — 56
Dabchick — 34
Darter, African — 35
Dikkop, Spotted — 47
Dikkop, Water — 47
Dove, Cape Turtle — 54
Dove, Greenspotted — 55
Dove, Laughing — 54
Dove, Mourning — 54
Dove, Namaqua — 55
Dove, Redeyed — 54
Drongo, Forktailed — 69
Duck, Knobbilled — 42
Duck, Whitebacked — 43
Duck, Whitefaced — 43
Duck, Yellowbilled — 43
Eagle, African Fish — 49
Eagle, Martial — 49
Eagle, Tawny — 50
Eagle, Wahlberg's — 50
Egret, Black — 38
Egret, Cattle — 37
Egret, Great White — 37
Egret, Little — 37
Egret, Slaty — 38
Falcon, Rednecked — 51
Finch, Melba — 83
Finch, Scalyfeathered — 81
Firefinch, Brown — 82
Firefinch, Redbilled — 82
Flycatcher, Black — 69
Flycatcher, Marico — 70
Flycatcher, Paradise — 70
Flycatcher, Spotted — 70
Francolin, Crested — 52
Francolin, Redbilled — 52
Francolin, Swainson's — 52
Gallinule, Purple — 44
Goose, Egyptian — 42
Goose, Pygmy — 42
Goose, Spurwinged — 42
Goshawk, Gabar — 51
Grebe, Little — 34
Guineafowl, Helmeted — 52
Gymnogene — 49
Hamerkop — 39
Harrier, African Marsh — 50
Helmetshrike, Redbilled — 75
Helmetshrike, White — 75
Heron, Blackcrowned Night — 36
Heron, Goliath — 36
Heron, Greenbacked — 38
Heron, Grey — 36
Heron, Purple — 36
Heron, Rufousbellied — 38
Heron, Squacco — 37
Honeyguide, Greater — 66
Hoopoe — 61
Hornbill, Bradfield's — 62
Hornbill, Ground — 53
Hornbill, Grey — 62
Hornbill, Redbilled — 62
Hornbill, Yellowbilled — 62
Ibis, Glossy — 39
Ibis, Hadeda — 39
Ibis, Sacred — 39
Jacana, African — 44
Jacana, Lesser — 44
Kestrel, Dickinson's — 51
Kingfisher, Giant — 58
Kingfisher, Malachite — 58
Kingfisher, Pied — 58
Kingfisher, Striped — 59
Kingfisher, Woodland — 59
Kite, Blackshouldered — 51
Kite, Yellowbilled — 50
Korhaan, Redcrested — 53
Lark, Rufousnaped — 66
Lourie, Grey — 56
Martin, Brownthroated — 65
Mousebird, Redfaced — 58
Nightjar, Fierynecked — 53
Oriole, Blackheaded — 65
Ostrich — 34
Owl, Barred — 57
Owl, Giant Eagle — 57
Owl, Pearlspotted — 57
Owl, Pel's Fishing — 57
Owl, Scops — 57
Oxpecker, Redbilled — 77
Oxpecker, Yellowbilled — 77
Parrot, Meyer's — 55
Pelican, Eastern White — 35
Pelican, Pinkbacked — 35
Pigeon, African Green — 55
Pipit, Grassland — 66
Pipit, Richard's — 66
Plover, Blacksmith — 46
Plover, Crowned — 46

Plover, Longtoed 46
Plover, Threebanded 45
Plover, Wattled 46
Pratincole, Redwinged 47
Prinia, Tawnyflanked 73
Puffback 75
Quelea, Redbilled 80
Robin, Heuglin's 68
Robin, Whitebrowed Scrub 68
Roller, Broadbilled 59
Roller, Lilacbreasted 59
Sandgrouse, Doublebanded 54
Sandpiper, Common 45
Sandpiper, Wood 45
Secretarybird 48
Shrike, Crimsonbreasted 76
Shrike, Longtailed 77
Shrike, Redbacked 76
Shrike, Whitecrowned 76
Skimmer, African 47
Sparrow, Greyheaded 79
Sparrow-weaver, Whitebrowed 79
Spoonbill, African 35
Starling, Burchell's 78
Starling, Glossy 78
Starling, Greater Blue-eared 78
Starling, Longtailed 78
Starling, Plumcoloured 78
Starling, Wattled 77
Stilt, Blackwinged 45
Stork, Abdim's 41
Stork, Marabou 40
Stork, Openbilled 41
Stork, Saddlebilled 40
Stork, White 40
Stork, Whitebellied 41
Stork, Woollynecked 41
Stork, Yellowbilled 40
Sunbird, Collared 74
Sunbird, Marico 74
Sunbird, Scarletchested 74
Sunbird, Whitebellied 74
Swallow, European 64
Swallow, Greyrumped 64
Swallow, Lesser Striped 64
Swallow, Wiretailed 64
Swift, Palm 65
Teal, Redbilled 43
Tern, Whiskered 47
Tern, Whitewinged 47
Thrush, Groundscraper 68
Thrush, Kurrichane 68
Tit, Southern Black 69
Vulture, Hooded 48
Vulture, Lappetfaced 48
Vulture, Whitebacked 48
Wagtail, African Pied 71
Wagtail, Cape 71
Warbler, African Marsh 72
Warbler, African Sedge 72
Warbler, Cape Reed 72
Warbler, Greater Swamp 72
Warbler, Greybacked Bleating 71
Warbler, Willow 73
Waxbill, Blue 83
Waxbill, Common 83
Waxbill, Violeteared 83
Weaver, Golden 81
Weaver, Lesser Masked 81
Weaver, Masked 81

Weaver, Spottedbacked 81
Weaver, Thickbilled 79
Weaver, Redheaded 80
White-eye, Yellow 73
Whydah, Paradise 82
Whydah, Pintailed 82
Widow, Redshouldered 80
Woodhoopoe, Redbilled 61
Woodpecker, Bearded 63
Woodpecker, Cardinal 63

REPTILES
Adder, Puff 88
Agama, Ground 90
Boomslang 87
Chameleon, Flapnecked 90
Cobra, Mozambique Spitting 88
Crocodile, Nile 85
Egg-eater, Common 86
House Snake, Brown 85
Gecko, Cape Dwarf 90
Gecko, Moreau's Tropical
House 90
Grass Snake, Olive 86
Lizard, Bushveld 89
Lizard, Common Roughscaled 89
Mamba, Black 88
Monitor, Rock 89
Monitor, Water 89
Python, African Rock 85
Sand Snake, Stripebellied 86
Skink, Striped 89
Skink, Variegated 89
Snake, Bark 86
Snake, Eastern Tiger 88
Snake, Mopane 86
Snake, Spotted Bush 87
Snake, Tree 87
Snake, Twig 87
Snake, Western Green 87
Snake, Vine 87
Terrapin, Okavango Hinged 85
Tortoise, Leopard 84
Tortoise, Serrated 84

FROGS
Bullfrog, Giant 91
Caco, Common 94
Foamnest Frog 93
Grass Frog, Mascarene 93
Grass Frog, Sharpnosed 93
Kassina, Bubbling 94
Platanna, Common 91
Rain Frog, Bushveld 93
Reed Frog, Long 94
Reed Frog, Painted 94
Rubber Frog, Banded 92
Shovelnosed Frog, Mottled 92
Toad, Guttural 92
Toad, Olive 92

FRESHWATER FISHES
Bottlenose, Western 95
Bulldog 95
Barb, Dashtail 96
Barbel 99
Barbel, Butter 99
Catfish, Sharptooth 99
Catfish, Silver 99
Cichlid, Jewel 97

Climbing Perch, Manyspined 99
Jewelfish, Banded 97
Mouthbrooder, Southern 97
Nembwe 98
Pike, African 97
Robber, Striped 96
Spiny Eel, Longtailed 96
Squeaker, Finetooth 99
Tigerfish 97
Tilapia, Banded 98
Tilapia, Redbreasted 98
Tilapia, Threespot 98
Topminnow, Johnston's 96

INVERTEBRATES
Freshwater shrimps 101
Insects
  Ants 104
  Beetles, Dung 103
  Butterflies
    African Monarch 105
    African Migrant 105
    Charaxes, Whitebarred 105
    White, Brownveined 105
  Cicadas 103
  Damselflies 102
  Dragonflies 102
  Flies, Blow 104
  Flies, Tsetse 104
  Grasshoppers 104
  Honey bees 104
  Moth, Lunar 105
  Moth, Mopane Emperor 105
  Mosquitoes 103
  Pond skaters 103
  Praying mantids 103
  Stick insects 103
  Termites 104
Leeches 100
Millipedes 101
River crabs 101
Scorpions 101
Snails, Water 100
Solifuges 101
Spiders
  Baboon 102
  Fish-eating 102
  Jumping 102
  Orb-web 102
Ticks 101

PLANTS
Abrus precatorius 118
Acacia erioloba 108
Acacia hebeclada 108
Acacia nigrescens 108
Acacia sieberiana 109
Acacia tortilis 109
Adansonia digitata 113
Albizia harveyi 108
Albizia, Sickleleaved 108
Asclepias fruticosa 118
Baikiaea plurijuga 110
Baobab 113
Baphia massaiensis 117
Bauhinia petersiana 117
Bauhinia, White 117
Berchemia discolor 112
Boscia albitrunca 107
Brandybush 116

Brasenia schreberi	119	Grass, Miscanthus	121	Rain Tree	111
Brown Ivory	112	Grass, Spike	121	Reed, Common	121
Buffalothorn	112	*Grewia flava*	116	Sand Camwood	117
Bulrush	120	Guarri, Magic	116	*Sansevieria aethiopica*	120
Burkea africana	109	*Hyphaene petersiana*	106	*Salvinia molesta*	120
Bushwillow, Russet	114	Jackalberry	113	Sausage Tree	115
Camelfoot	110	Kalahari Currant	116	Savanna Gardenia	117
Camelthorn	108	Kariba Weed	120	*Schinziophyton rautanenii*	111
Camwood, Sand	117	Kiaat	110	*Sclerocarya birrea*	112
Candlepod Acacia	108	*Kigelia africana*	115	Shepherd's Tree	107
Caperbush, Woolly	116	*Kirkia accuminata*	117	Sicklebush	109
Capparis tomentosa	116	Knobthorn	108	Sourplum, Large	116
Carissa edulis	116	Large Sourplum	116	*Sporobolus spicatus*	121
Climbing Numnum	116	Lavendar Feverberry	117	Star Apple, Red	116
Colophospermum mopane	110	Leadwood	114	Sundew	120
Combretum celastroides	114	*Leonotis nepetifolia*	118	Swamp Fern	120
Combretum hereroense	114	*Lonchocarpus capassa*	111	Syringa, White	117
Combretum imberbe	114	Luckybean Creeper	118	Syringa, Wild	109
Combretum, Jessebush	114	Magic Guarri	116	*Syzygium cordatum*	113
Combretum, Knobbly	114	Mahogany, Natal	115	Teak, Zambezi	110
Combretum mossambicense	114	Mangosteen, African	113	*Terminalia prunioides*	115
Confetti Tree	112	Manketti	111	Terminalia, Purplepod	115
Croton gratissimus	117	Marula	112	*Terminalia sericea*	115
Croton megalobotrys	111	*Maytenus senegalensis*	112	Terminalia, Silver	115
Cynodon dactylon	121	Milkweed	118	*Thelypterus interrupta*	120
Cyperus papyrus	121	*Miscanthus junceus*	121	*Trapa natans*	119
Dichrostachys cinerea	109	Mistletoe	120	Tree Vernonia	117
Diospyros lycioides	116	Mopane	110	*Trichilia emetica*	115
Diospyros mespiliformis	113	Mother-in-law's Tongue	120	*Typha capensis*	120
Dissotis canescens	118	Numnum, Climbing	117	Umbrellathorn	109
Drosera madagascariensis	120	*Nymphaea lotus*	119	*Vernonia amygdalina*	117
Eichhornia crassipes	120	*Nymphaea nouchali caerulea*	119	Vernonia, Tree	117
Euclea divinorum	116	*Nymphoides indica*	119	Waterberry	113
Feverberry, Large	111	*Ottelia ulvifolia*	119	Water Chestnut	119
Ficus burkei	107	Palm, Fan	106	Water Gentian	119
Ficus sycomorus	107	Palm, Ivory	106	Water Hyacinth	120
Ficus thonningii	107	Palm, Wild Date	106	Water Lettuce	119
Ficus verruculosa	107	Paperbark Acacia	109	Water Shield	119
Fig, Common Wild	107	Papyrus	121	Waterlily, Day	119
Fig, Sycamore	107	*Phoenix reclinata*	106	Waterlily, Night	119
Fig, Water	107	*Phragmites australis*	121	Wild Dagga	118
Garcinia livingstonei	113	*Phyllanthus reticulatus*	111	Wild Tibouchina	118
Gardenia, Savanna	117	*Piliostigma thonningii*	110	*Ximenia caffra*	116
Gardenia volkensii	117	Potatobush	111	Zambezi Teak	110
Grass, Couch	121	*Pterocarpus angolensis*	110	*Ziziphus mucronata*	112